Finding and Keeping the Right People

■ ■ ■

About the Author

Jon Billsberry is a lecturer in Organisational Behaviour at the Open University Business School. He is the course team chair of *The Effective Manager*, one of Europe's largest management courses.

Before turning to academia, he spent six years as a manager in the manufacturing and financial services industries and spent four years as a headhunter with Scott Collins Ltd.

The Institute of Management (IM) is at the forefront of management development and best management practice. The Institute embraces all levels of management from students to chief executives. It provides a unique portfolio of services for all managers, enabling them to develop skills and achieve management excellence.

If you would like to hear more about the benefits of membership, please write to Department P, Institute of Management, Cottingham Road, Corby NN17 1TT.

This series is commissioned by the Institute of Management Foundation.

Finding and Keeping the Right People

How to recruit motivated employees

■ ■ ■

JON BILLSBERRY

the Institute of Management

FOUNDATION

PITMAN PUBLISHING

London · Hong Kong · Johannesburg
Melbourne · Singapore · Washington DC

PITMAN PUBLISHING
128 Long Acre, London WC2E 9AN
Tel: +44 (0) 171 447 2000
Fax: +44 (0) 171 240 5771

A Division of Pearson Professional Limited

First published in Great Britain 1996

© Pearson Professional Limited 1996

British Library Cataloguing in Publication Data
A CIP catalogue record for this book can be obtained from the British Library.

ISBN 0 273 61698 6

10 9 8 7 6 5 4 3 2 1

Typeset by Northern Phototypesetting Co Ltd, Bolton
Printed and bound in Great Britain by Bell and Bain Ltd, Glasgow

The Publishers' policy is to use paper manufactured from sustainable forests.

Contents

■ ■ ■

Foreword

■ ■ ■

Jon Billsberry's latest book breaks new ground as a practical text. It admits in public what a lot of employers have been saying in private: the fit of an individual employee with the organisation is just as important as their fit to the job.

As information and restructuring revolutionise the nature of jobs, it becomes ever more difficult to describe them in terms of a set of tasks. The knowledge and skills necessary for the job can thus no longer be so clearly specified. With employees being expected to take more responsibility for day to day decisions, the criteria are now about values and attitudes which are in tune with the organisation's overall direction and culture. Competitive performance derives from the application of these values to one's work.

Unlike many writers on recruitment and selection, Jon takes the process as a whole, stressing the need for integration and continuously remembering the fundamental business purpose of the exercise. He looks at recruitment and selection from the practitioner's perspective, which is why he includes a chapter on legal aspects. This is a book for the personnel coal face, but it's the coal face of the future rather than the old seams of the past.

Peter Herriot
Institute of Employment Studies

Acknowledgements

■ ■ ■

I should like to thank Véronique Ambrosini, Timothy Clark, Peter Herriot, Romas Kusneraitis and Philip Marsh for their helpful comments and advice. Of course, the errors, omissions and views expressed in this book are entirely the responsibility of the author.

Introduction

■ ■ ■

The most important and expensive decisions in organisations are the least carefully considered. They are taken without any analysis of the problem. They are taken without any evidence to support the decision. They are taken by people who have no responsibility for the consequences. And they are taken on the authority of just one person's gut feeling. What are these decisions? As you've probably guessed, these are recruitment and selection decisions.

You might have heard it said that every recruitment decision is a million pound decision. This is more accurate than you might think. Imagine that a person stays twenty five years with your organisation and that their average salary over this period is £20,000. The person will cost the organisation £500,000 in salary alone at today's prices. This ignores the ancillary costs of employer's national insurance contributions, training, stationery, equipment, and so on which are usually thought to double the salary costs of employing someone. In addition, a full costing would include the consequences of the many actions that the person makes and the opportunity costs of the things the person decided not to do. This might be called the 'Baring's Factor'.

Even when you recruit on a short term contract, say for three years, the costs quickly mount up. For example, if you recruit someone for three years at £17,000, the salary cost is £51,000. If you double this to take account of the ancillary costs, then it becomes a £102,000 decision.

Many writers say that organisations are no more than the people that comprise them. The organisation, so they say, is merely a collection of individuals who have come together to pursue a common goal. There is much truth in this, for without people most organisations would not exist. People make decisions. People produce finished products. People design marketing campaigns. People sell things. People put together the accounts. Viewed in this way, the decision to recruit someone is not just a big financial decision, it is also one that will determine the future of the organisation.

Why do I say that recruitment and selection decisions are the least carefully considered? For a moment think back to the last time you recruited someone. How much time did you spend analysing the job and the ways that it might develop? How much time did you spend considering different ways to attract a pool of candidates? How much time did you spend preparing questions to test for the knowledge, skills and abilities that you were looking for? How much time did you spend interviewing the successful candidate? How much time did you spend thinking about your decision?

If you're anything like the vast majority of managers in the UK, you probably spent fewer than ten hours in total. Compare that to the time you spend on other tasks and decisions.

RECRUITMENT DECISIONS ARE BIG DECISIONS

1 The organisation is committed to long-standing salary payments.
2 The organisation incurs many ancillary costs.
3 Bad decisions lead to the recruitment of people who perform poorly and who, in turn, make further poor decisions.
4 Recruitment decisions dictate the future direction of the organisation.

It's 9.15 am in the finance department of a small building society. The department manager has just switched on her computer and settled down with a cup of coffee to check the month's management accounts. John walks into her office.

'Can I have a word please, Pascale?'

Pascale smiles and points to the chair. 'What is it now?', she thinks.

'I'm afraid I've got some bad news for you; I'm leaving. I'll work out my notice as well as I can, of course.'

Pascale is shell-shocked. Eventually she says, 'You've only been here five months, what's wrong? Why are you leaving? ... where are you going? Can we do anything to keep you?'

'It's nothing personal, but I just don't think I fit in around here. I'm going to 'temp' a bit until I find something else.'

A few pleasantries are exchanged and then John returns to his desk to begin working out his notice.

After a few moments, Pascale picks up the phone and calls Rob, the company's Human Resources Manager. 'Are you free? I've got a problem; John's just resigned. I need to get a replacement fast as the year end's almost upon us.'

By 9.40 am Pascale and Rob are discussing what to do. 'The problem is that I need someone who can do the job fast. John leaving now is a disaster.'

'What about promoting Chris, Roger or Jaswinder? They're up to it aren't they?'

'Sure, but they're indispensable in their current jobs. Replacing them would be an even worse nightmare. It would take ages to train anyone to do their jobs. No, I can't promote them. Look, all I need is someone who understands basic bookkeeping, who can reconcile a bank account and has some supervisory experience in an accounts department. It didn't take us long to recruit John last time, let's do the same again.'

'OK, I'll ring round the local agencies and ask them to send in some CVs.'

A couple of days later, Rob is confronted with a large pile of CVs from four local agencies. He picks up the phone, 'Pascale, you've got to help me; I'm not sure what you want.'

Pascale joins Rob and they begin to search through the pile. 'No ... no ... yes ... no ... yes ... no ... Some of these are OK.'

Pascale hands Rob a pile of eleven CVs. 'Could you call these in for us to see? They seem to have the sort of skills we need.'

'When are you free to see them?'

'Tomorrow afternoon and early evening, and the day after.'

'Yes, I'm free then as well. Would you prefer to see them together or separately?'

'I think, perhaps, separately. That'll give us the chance to form separate opinions, won't it? Bill will need to approve our choice as well. I'll check his availability once we've picked the best.'

Of the eleven, nine are happy to be interviewed and they troop in over the next two days. First they see Rob and then, after a five minute break, they see Pascale. Both interviews last about 45 minutes. After they've seen all the candidates, Rob and Pascale meet to decide who to select.

'How should we do this?' asks Pascale.

'Well, we need to compare them with each other and also against what you need. How about we write all the names up on the whiteboard and analyse each one against all of your needs?'

Pascale nods her approval and Rob writes the names of every applicant horizontally across the whiteboard. 'Right, so what must they be able to do?'

'Be experienced in supervising staff, reconciling bank accounts, have knowledge of purchase and sales ledgers, preparing management accounts, basic financial accounting, fixed assets, be able to use our spreadsheets – and some forecasting experience would be useful. Oh, they must fit in as well.'

For the following hour, Rob and Pascale struggle to remember each of the candidates clearly. They find that there seems to be very little difference between any of the applicants.

'The problem is,' says Rob, 'almost all of them appear to be competent accountants, but we've no real evidence to suggest that they can do the job well. We've only eliminated three as less suitable than the others. Who do you think will fit in best?'

'Tough question. Perhaps the chap from the credit card company. It seems a similar sort of place and the work's also similar. I thought the girl with the red hair would get on with people in the department. She had a good sense of humour. I suppose these are the ones I'd put first.'

'Right, I don't disagree. To tell you the truth, I think that they're all a little dull and lifeless. But we've got to make a decision and those two did seem the best of the bunch. Shall we arrange for them to see Bill as soon as possible?'

The two candidates, Nick and Juliet, see Bill the following day for a thirty minute interview. He prefers Nick and thinks that his experience from the credit card company will be useful. Bill, Pascale and Rob meet and decide to offer the job to Nick. They agree that, at a pinch, Juliet would also be acceptable.

Nick refuses the job. He tells Rob that he was a little unimpressed with the people he met at the two interviews. As Pascale is desperate to get someone, they decide to offer the job to Juliet. She accepts and Rob writes to the referees to check her suitability. Glowing references are returned and a start date is agreed in four weeks time which, unfortunately, coincides with Pascale's two week holiday.

'It's OK, Roger and Jaswinder can show her the ropes until I get back.'

Six weeks pass and Pascale returns from holiday. A post-it note on her desk from Rob says, 'Please come and see me as soon as you get in'. Pascale wonders what the problem is and goes to see him.

'We've got a problem. Last Friday, Roger resigned. He's really pissed off. I don't think Jaswinder's very happy either.'

'What's happened? What's wrong?'

'It seems that they're both annoyed with the recruitment of Juliet. They've both told me that they thought they should have got John's job. Roger said that Juliet is no more experienced than he.

By the way, I think Chris wants a word with you as well and you should have a word with Juliet. As you can imagine she's feeling a little unnerved. On top of everything else, I think that she's having some difficulties adjusting to our culture.'

Now, put yourself in Pascale's place. How would you have found a replacement for John? What would you have done? Do you think you would have avoided the mistakes that Pascale made?

What will this book do for you?

The case study you've just read highlights many of the mistakes typically made by managers who have little training in recruitment and selection. Perhaps the greatest error that Pascale and Rob made was not to give recruitment and selection its due. They did not realise its importance. They also made many omissions. For example, they didn't conduct a job analysis, and therefore, they couldn't list the competencies that applicants would need to be successful in the job. They failed to consider the development of existing staff, they failed to consider the needs of each of the applicants, and they failed to consider objectively how each of the applicants would fit with the organisation's culture.

By the end of this book, I hope that you will be able to return to this case study and identify more mistakes that both Pascale and Rob made. Not only should you be able to identify the mistakes, you should also know how to develop and carry out recruitment and selection in a way that prevents you making these same mistakes.

> ### BOOK OBJECTIVES
>
> When you have read this book, you should be able to:
> - operate all aspects of the recruitment and selection process effectively
> - avoid unfair discrimination
> - analyse the job that you are trying to fill
> - analyse the qualities that people must have to be able to fit in
> - choose appropriate techniques for attracting a pool of candidates
> - manage the work of third party recruitment agents
> - choose appropriate selection techniques
> - interview fairly and objectively
> - design an effective introduction
> - help newcomers adjust to the new organisation
> - manage the careers of newcomers
> - evaluate the effectiveness of your organisational entry process.

The style and structure of this book

This book is designed to be as interactive as possible. The interaction helps you in several ways:

- to internalise the ideas by giving you time to reflect
- to check that you have understood the ideas
- to see the relevance of the ideas to your own job
- to make the text more varied and, therefore, more interesting.

The interaction takes two forms:

- reflections or exercises
- activities.

Most of the exercises give you the opportunity to relate the ideas in the book to your own situation. Others pause you so that you can reflect on the material covered. Usually there is feedback following each reflection or exercise. The activities serve a different purpose. They form a practical series of tasks which, if followed through, will help you to find a new employee.

How you might use this book

I have written this book for two types of people:

Managers who have very little experience of recruiting staff

Every aspect of recruitment and selection, from the initial identification that you need to find someone all the way through to techniques to help integrate the newcomer into the job and the organisation, is considered. Each chapter examines an important part of the process and shows you how to be effective. By the time you have read all the book, you should be able to perform every stage.

Experienced recruiters who want specific help

You might be a manager experienced in recruiting staff. If so, this book will still be of value to you. Recently, there have been many developments to the theory underpinning recruitment and selection, many of which are included. One of them, for example, is the need to assess applicants on job related and organisational criteria. If you want to use this book to update yourself, or to get remedial help with certain aspects of the recruitment and selection process, I advise you to complete the self assessment exercise at the end of this chapter and read the following chapter. This will highlight those areas on which you need to concentrate. Of course, there is nothing to stop you reading the whole book!

Why do we need another book on recruitment and selection?

This book takes a different approach to every other book I know on recruitment and selection. Other books concentrate on the assessment of the knowledge, skills and abilities of applicants that are important if the new employee is to perform effectively in the job. While this is an important consideration, I believe that the fit of a person to a job is only part of the decision that selectors must make: they also have to assess how each applicant will fit in with the organisation's culture, subcultures, values, goals and people. There is no point identifying which applicant has the best skills to do the job, if that applicant cannot function in the new organisation.

In this book, I show how you can assess applicants for their fit to the job and to the organisation. It is the first practical book incorporating both these considerations.

Self diagnosis exercise

Use these questions to see which parts of the book you need to study.

	True	False
1 Recruitment is choosing between candidates	❏	❏
2 Introduction is helping the newcomer adapt to the organisation	❏	❏
3 3% of your workforce must be disabled	❏	❏
4 You can discriminate against gay applicants	❏	❏
5 You can discriminate against married applicants	❏	❏
6 You can discriminate against single applicants	❏	❏
7 Ex-offenders can deny they've been in prison	❏	❏
8 Recruitment starts with job analysis	❏	❏
9 Recruitment ends when you offer someone a job	❏	❏
10 Corporate advertising in job adverts helps	❏	❏
11 You should only analyse the job	❏	❏
12 Selection criteria are the factors used to assess the suitability of candidates	❏	❏
13 Formal training is required to analyse jobs	❏	❏
14 New jobs should be analysed as well as existing jobs	❏	❏
15 You should exclude factors relating to the organisation's culture when analysing jobs	❏	❏
16 The purpose of adverts is to attract as many applicants as possible	❏	❏
17 Work with headhunters is managed with a contract	❏	❏
18 Intelligence and analogous tests are the best ways to assess applicants	❏	❏
19 References should be requested before interviewing	❏	❏
20 A verbal offer of a job is binding on the organisation	❏	❏
21 You have 13 weeks to send newcomers a contract of employment	❏	❏

22 The introduction to work begins on the first day of
employment ❏ ❏

23 Reducing stress is a key part of recruitment ❏ ❏

24 Buddying is the process of helping newcomers
make friends at work ❏ ❏

25 Managing careers is a good way to keep people ❏ ❏

26 Before recruiting new staff you should analyse
previous organisational entry exercises ❏ ❏

Answers

1–2	Both false (chapter 1)
3–7	True until the new Disability Act comes into force, true, false, true, true (chapter 2)
8–9	Both false (chapter 3)
10	False (chapter 4)
11–15	False, true, false, true, false (chapter 5)
16–17	False, true (chapter 6)
18–19	True (sometimes), false (chapter 7)
20–21	Both true (chapter 8)
22–23	Fairly true, true (chapter 9)
24	False (chapter 10)
25	True (chapter 11)
26	True (chapter 12)

MEMORANDUM

To: Joe Longley
Personnel Director

Date: 26/09/96

From: Elaine Hurst
Marketing Director

Re: Retaining staff

Joe,

As you know, I've been on your interviewing training course. I also make sure that I apply the ideas when I'm interviewing for real. With this new upwards appraisal system, I think I now know that I'm a reasonable manager. So why does every new recruit I employ leave within six months? It's happened four times now.

I've looked back at the records and I'm convinced that I analysed the job properly and picked the person with the best skills and knowledge. What can I do to make sure this doesn't happen again?

Regards,

Elaine

MEMORANDUM

To: Elaine Hurst   **Date:** 29/09/96
     Marketing Director

From: Joe Longley
       Personnel Director

Re: Retaining staff

Elaine,

Thanks for bringing this to my attention. It does seem a problem. I got my old Personnel Management textbooks out and tried to find where you'd gone wrong. According to them, you did everything right.

To find a solution, I phoned a lecturer from the Open University I met at a conference earlier in the year. He suggested that the old books only looked at half the story as they tend to ignore how people fit into their environment at work. He said this factor is strongly linked to people's satisfaction, commitment and likelihood of leaving. He also said that most organisations only think about what's best for them – you know, has the applicant got the right skills, knowledge, level of motivation and so on? – without considering what's best for the applicant. So people get recruited when it's not necessarily in their best interests. No wonder then that people leave after a few months if they can't stand the environment or the people they work with.

Instead, he says that we should try to understand the environment that people have to work in. And then suss out what it is that people need to be able to cope with it. After all, why do people leave? It's not because they can't do the job, or because they like changing companies. In fact, changing companies is stressful. It's whether they get on with people, whether they agree with the values of the place; those sorts of things. And these are things we could measure and assess when interviewing.

In essence, he's saying that when we recruit people we should think about it from their point of view. And that means thinking about how they'll fit in.

He's sent me a book that contains his ideas. Copy enclosed. It's called *Finding and Keeping the Right People*. I've had a look through it and it seems most exciting. There's a whole section on how you go about understanding the environment in which people work. I hope it's of help.

Regards,

Joe

1

■ ■ ■

What are the ideas behind organisational entry?

CHAPTER OBJECTIVES

After reading this chapter, you should be able to:

- describe the 'traditional' approach to recruitment and selection and be able to argue why it is an incomplete approach
- define the terms 'selection', 'recruitment', 'organisational entry', and 'introduction'
- say what you hope to achieve when recruiting new staff
- describe the different types of 'fit' that you are trying to assess when looking for new staff.

CHAPTER OVERVIEW

In this chapter, I explain the relevant theory underlying recruitment and selection. I look at the traditional approach to recruitment and selection which puts emphasis on the selection stage of the process. Then I look at an alternative approach which considers a much larger process that begins when you recognise there's a need to find someone and ends when the newcomer has adapted to the organisation and is performing effectively. I propose that new recruits must 'fit' the job and the organisation in a number of ways: they must be able to fit with the organisation's culture, and they must also have the knowledge, skills and abilities to do the job well.

Some definitions
■ ■ ■

Before I begin, I should first define a few terms. Some of the terms in common usage actually have specific meanings, such as recruitment, selection and induction. I need to explain my understanding and usage of these words so that we are on the same wavelength.

Organisational entry

So far in this book, I have referred to the 'recruitment and selection' process. I have used this term because it is the one most commonly used by managers. However, the words 'recruitment' and 'selection' have specific meanings and using them to describe the whole process seduces the reader into thinking that the process ends when you have decided whom to employ. This is wrong. The process of the entry of an individual into an organisation ends when the newcomer is fully integrated into that organisation and performing effectively. Consequently, I shall use the term 'organisational entry' when I want to refer to the whole process of finding new staff and integrating them into the organisation.

Recruitment

The word 'recruitment' refers specifically to the attraction of a pool of candidates and the processes associated with this. In particular, recruitment refers to the decision on how to attract candidates, the design of advertisements, the management of external consultants and the administration of the organisational entry process.

Unfortunately there isn't a verb to cover the whole organisational entry process or the process of filling a vacancy. But the common usage of 'to recruit' does have this meaning. So, when I talk about the need to recruit someone, I am referring to the whole organisational entry process or the need to find someone to fill a particular role or vacancy. 'Recruitment' as a noun has a different and specific meaning. I'll use 'to attract' as the verb when talking about the recruitment phase of organisational entry.

> **RECRUITMENT is the process of attracting suitably qualified people to apply for the position.**

Selection

The word 'selection' refers specifically to the process of choosing between applicants. This occurs at several stages in the organisational entry process. For example, when choosing whom to shortlist, whom to interview a second time, and whom to employ.

> **SELECTION is the process of assessing applicants and choosing whom to employ.**

Introduction

Induction is a vague term that can be used in a number of ways. Generally, it is used to refer to the first week or so of a person's employment in a new organisation. To avoid this imprecision, I shall use the word 'introduction' to refer specifically to the newcomer's first day at work and the preparation for the first day. Introduction has two purposes:

3

- to help newcomers overcome the stress of starting a new job
- to introduce newcomers to the requirements of the job.

> **INTRODUCTION is the process of helping the newcomer survive their first day at work.**

What does recruitment mean to you?
■ ■ ■

In this book, I want to outline a new approach to the recruitment and selection of staff and show how you can use these ideas to make your own organisational entry much more effective. Before I begin to discuss the various techniques that you can use, I must first dispel a few myths.

The traditional approach to recruitment and selection

For almost a century, researchers, academics and psychologists have argued that the purpose of organisational entry is to find someone who can do the job well. The effectiveness of these practices is judged by examining newcomers' subsequent job performance. Good performance, it has long been believed, is a function of the knowledge, skills, abilities and other characteristics (KSAOs) that newcomers possess and the demands of the job. As a result, managers wanting to find a new member of staff are told to conduct a job analysis and from this extrapolate the KSAOs that a newcomer must possess. The KSAOs are used in the recruitment process to design an advertisement or brief an agency, and they are also used in the selection process as the criteria to judge applicants.

However, in the past ten or so years, many people have become increasingly dissatisfied with this approach to organisational entry. There are several reasons why it is now regarded as less than perfect.

- The pace of change in the business environment is now so rapid, with the development of new technologies, processes, practices and the like, that a job description derived from a job analysis quickly becomes dated. Therefore, many people are employed to do jobs that are not what they, or the organisation, expected them to be.

- This approach assumes that the behaviour of people is stable and consistent regardless of the environment in which they find themselves. Research has shown this to be only partly true. In addition, people interact with and change the situations that they experience. So, when looking for someone to employ, you need to take account of how the person will change and react to the job, and also how the person will change and react to the environment in which they will work.

- This approach to recruitment and selection is more concerned with finding new employees than with keeping them. As a result, it does little to assess the potential dissatisfaction or stress that newcomers will experience in the job. These are important factors for high performance and are, of course, factors we should be seeking to minimise wherever possible. Furthermore, these factors are linked to greater staff turnover which is, again, something organisations want to avoid if possible.

- Introduction to the new job and socialisation are rarely considered as part of the organisational entry process even though they are important factors determining the success of new recruits.

- The traditional approach only considers recruitment and selection from the organisation's point of view. It fails to acknowledge that applicants make decisions as well. Applicants make some vital decisions: they decide whether to leave their current job; whether to apply for the job you are advertising; whether to attend an interview or whether to do your tests; and whether to accept the job if it's offered.

4

- Despite the fact that this approach has long been advocated by many people, it has not become the accepted method to recruit new staff. If it had, we should expect tests, such as intelligence tests and work sample tests, to dominate selection and the unstructured interview would be used very rarely. In fact, the opposite is true. Survey after survey has shown that organisations choose to use unstructured interviews in preference to supposedly more valid and reliable tests. Why is this? How can this be explained?

- At present, the most convincing explanation is that the traditional approach to selection is only partly appropriate and that other issues, such as the candidate's fit to the organisation and current staff, are assessed by interviewers.

What are you trying to achieve when you decide to recruit new staff?

When you read the above points, do they strike a chord with you? Do they reflect your own experience of finding new staff? When you look for new staff what are you trying to achieve? What are your objectives?

5

A new approach to organisational entry
■ ■ ■

Perhaps the greatest problem with the traditional approach to organisational entry is the fact that managers end up thinking 'how can I find someone to do this job?'. This one-sided approach is doomed to failure as it only considers one of the factors leading to better performance. Instead, try thinking about organisational entry in the following way: 'how well do each of the candidates fit with the job and the organisation?'.

I hope you can see that by thinking about organisational entry in terms of how people will fit, you will consider a broader range of managerial issues. No longer are you thinking that you have *carte blanche* to take whatever decisions you like. No longer is organisational entry a one-sided process where you pick whom you want from the pool of applicants with little regard to the consequences. Instead, you try to find a fit that is suited to the individual, the organisation, and you as a manager. In this way, you increase the likelihood of finding someone who will not only perform well in the job, but is motivated to do the job well, committed to the organisation, and will gain satisfaction from the job.

In this book, I shall adopt this new approach. I shall try to explain how you can ensure that your selection decisions are based on the fit between the applicants and the job and the organisation.

What are the objectives of organisational entry?
■ ■ ■

Traditionally, the objectives of the organisational entry process are to locate and hire someone who can do a job well. The new 'fit' approach to organisational entry suggests that managers should think about a much greater number and diversity of objectives. This new approach seems to mirror the actual practice of managers better.

What are the objectives of organisational entry?

Think back to the case study in the Introduction, the one in which Pascale and Rob made such a mess of finding a new member of staff. What do you think were Pascale and Rob's objectives when they began to look for a new member of staff?

In retrospect, given the outcomes, what do you think they would now see as the objectives of organisational entry?

> At the start of the episode it seems that Pascale and Rob's objective was simply to find someone who had the skills to do the job. But by the end of the episode, I suspect that they wouldn't just say 'to get someone to do a job'. Instead, they would probably talk about the need to find someone who can fit in, contribute to the team effort and get satisfaction from their work. They might talk of the effect the newcomer has on other people and the need to help the person adjust to the new environment. They might also talk about the need to assess the skills and abilities of every applicant properly. Unfortunately, these objectives only became clear after they made such a mess of recruiting someone.

It seems that there are many different objectives of organisational entry. Some of the short term objectives are:

- to complete the process as quickly as possible
- to recruit and select fairly
- to recruit as inexpensively as possible without compromising the quality of the process
- to find someone to do a job that needs doing

- to find someone who won't disrupt the work or morale of existing members of staff
- to find someone who can be effective and contribute quickly
- to find someone who will need little training
- to manage the organisational entry process with minimal disruption to existing members of staff.

Some of the longer term objectives are:

- to introduce new competencies into the organisation
- to build an effective team
- to ensure that new employees can operate within the organisation's cultures and systems
- to lower the turnover of staff - i.e. more stable work force
- to find staff who will get satisfaction from their work
- to introduce people into the organisation who are 'in tune' with the organisation's mission, values, and goals.

These are just some of the objectives of organisational entry. Clearly, there are many others. However, even this relatively short list illustrates that organisational entry is more than simply finding someone to do a job – important though this is.

It is possible to reduce the objectives to just three underlying concerns:

- the efficient, fair and cost-effective administration of the entry process
- the examination of the fit of the individual and the job (I shall refer to this as 'job fit')
- the assessment of the fit between the individual and the organisation (I shall refer to this as 'organisation fit').

The efficient, fair and cost-effective administration of the entry process

Efficient administration

The efficient administration of organisational entry is important for two reasons:

- to minimise the time and money spent handling applications and candidates
- to project a positive image of the organisation.

As the administration underlies every part of the process, it is impractical to separate out all the administrative tasks. Therefore, I have opted to cover these points as I discuss each part of the organisational entry process.

Fair organisational entry

It almost goes without saying that all candidates need to be treated fairly. This is to everyone's benefit. Individual applicants benefit because their fit to the job and the organisation determine whether or not they get offered the job, rather than subjective judgement or manager's 'gut feel'. The organisation benefits because it wants to employ the person who best fits the job and the culture. Subjective and unfair discrimination reduces the likelihood of this happening.

There are also legal implications to organisational entry of which all recruiters should be aware. This topic is so important that I have devoted the whole of the next chapter to it.

Cost-effective organisational entry

8

A large body of research indicates that investment in organisational entry systems is one of the best investments an organisation can make. If the organisation gets it right, it employs its future senior managers, supervisors etc., and they gain valuable experience along the way. On the other hand, if the organisation gets it wrong, it has to spend additional money on further advertisements or consultants and then reinvest managerial time selecting and inducting newcomers. If people are recruited who fit neither the job nor the organisation well, dissatisfaction, stress and conflict are increased.

Cost effectiveness can be achieved in many ways. The following will all help to reduce the costs and maximise the benefits:

- getting it right first time
- using recruitment and selection techniques that yield appropriate outcomes
- automating as much of the system as possible without appearing impersonal.

These items are discussed throughout the book.

Job fit

One of the main purposes of this book is to show how considerations of organisation fit can be integrated into the organisational entry system. But in spite of this, fitting people to jobs is still a key ingredient in virtually every organisational entry system. It is essential to identify the knowledge, skills, abilities and other characteristics that candidates must possess for high performance. While people may grow out of and change jobs, it is essential that they can still perform the tasks and meet the objectives set by the organisation.

During the twentieth century, the assessment of job fit has become quite a refined science – well, compared to the assessment of organisation fit. Much has been written on the topic and there are many approaches to it. In chapter 5, I shall describe the way you can analyse jobs with a view to recruiting people for them. The techniques have one or more of three objectives. They seek to reveal:

- the **skills** needed to do the job
- the **tasks** that must be done, or
- the **objectives** to be met.

I shall show how you can analyse each of these to help you understand the type of person you need to do the job. I shall also show you how to construct the all-important 'selection criteria' derived from the job analysis (and the organisation analysis). These are the criteria upon which your selection decisions are made.

9

In chapter 7, the techniques available to you to determine the individual's fit to the job are examined. And I shall discuss how you can decide which techniques are appropriate and then how to operate each one.

Organisation fit

This book aims to integrate the new ideas about fitting people to organisations to the practical application of organisation entry policies. The basic idea behind organisation fit is that there is more to organisational entry than simply fitting people to jobs. Other factors such as an organisation's culture, systems, goals, values, and climate affect newcomers' performance, as does, of course, the way they interact with their colleagues.

What's it like to work in your organisation?

Organisational culture is one of those terms that can be quite difficult to understand. Later in the book I'll look at ways you can analyse the culture of your organisation. But before I move on, it's worth just spending a few moments to reflect on what your culture is. Imagine that a friend is thinking of coming to work at your organisation. 'Tell me what it's like to work there.' How would you reply?

The question 'what's it like to work in your organisation?' is quite a good way of getting at the organisation's culture. It's likely that you'd respond by describing how you get on with people, what the atmosphere's like, whether there are endless meetings, how you get promoted and so on. All of these combine to illustrate the pervasive context for everything that is thought and done in your organisation from your perspective. One word of caution. The term organisational culture is usually taken to refer to an agreed description of these things – not just one individual's way of seeing things. Ask yourself if others that you work with would agree with your description of what it's like to work in your organisation.

How often have you heard, or used, a phrase like, 'I don't really think she'll fit in, you know'. The difficulty with current assessments of organisational fit is that it is almost totally subjective. It is based on gut feelings, the personal likes and dislikes of interviewers, and guess-work. Consequently, the organisational fit criterion is frequently used to reject applicants when interviewers don't like them, albeit without realising that it is organisational fit they are referring to. This is a considerable barrier to fair organisational entry. In chapters 5 and 7, I shall discuss methods of **objectively** assessing the 'organisational fit' of candidates.

How 'fits' fit together

To recap, I have suggested that there are two types of 'fit' that recruiters need to assess:

- job fit
- organisational fit.

Applicants want to find out if the job is right for them. Have I got the right skills? Will it interest me? Is it beyond me? Will it bore me? And, applicants are very keen to find out if they will fit in. What are the people like? Can I get on with them? Will I make friends here?

On the other side of the coin, managers need to find out if applicants can do the job, or pick it up quickly. Have they the right skills? Is it sufficiently challenging for them? And, they need to know whether they will fit to the culture or can adapt to it. If not, they are likely to become dissatisfied, perform poorly and leave.

It seems, therefore, that both types of fit are important, and that there must be a fit between the individual and organisation on both counts. Failure in one domain will be a **critical fault** that prevents the **employee** performing well and gaining satisfaction from their work.

It naturally follows that, as a recruiter, you must assure yourself that anyone you appoint fits the job and the organisation.

It is easy to convince yourself that it is sensible to recruit someone who seems outstanding in one domain, but who fails in the other with a view that 'he'll adapt after he's been here a few months'. This is a mistaken view. Research has time and time again shown that round pegs don't fit into square holes.

Helena attended two interviews at a medium sized print company for the job of assistant buyer. At her interviews, everyone she met was most impressed and thought she would fit in well. She had been at school with several people in the department, played in the same hockey club as the department manager and had experience of printing from her college studies. Unfortunately, she had little experience of buying in a commercial environment. At the interview this was glossed over, *'I'm sure she'll pick it up quickly – purchasing's not that difficult'* said the department manager. Everyone was in agreement and she was offered the job.

After a couple of months it was clear that everything was not as it should be. Helena had settled in well with everyone and was keen to succeed. But she was not a buyer. She had problems with the numerical side of the job and was a poor negotiator. Even in the few things that she had purchased so far, it was clear that she had not achieved anything like the best deal and that, even with supportive colleagues and excellent training, she just wasn't cut out to be a buyer. Helena realised the situation and was very unhappy. She enjoyed working at the company, but wasn't enjoying the job itself. Something had to be done.

There followed a series of meetings involving the department manager, the sales manager, the personnel manager and Helena. They decided that Helena should move over to a job in the sales department and that the buying department should look for someone else. It took a further three months to recruit someone as a replacement. In all, the buying team had spent six months without an effective person in a key role. Morale had sunk, performance had fallen off, and buying contracts had been negotiated that committed the organisation to unfavourable arrangements for several years to come.

11

A pictorial summary of fitting fits together

Some of the ideas in this chapter might be quite new to you. It's possible to display the new ideas in a series of simple pictures. The first picture shows a situation where you might consider employing the applicant as they fit on both job and organisational aspects. The saw-tooth edge of the two fits represents the fact that job fit and organisational fit interact and influence each other.

Recruit this person

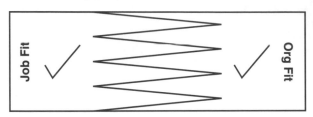

In the second picture, the applicant fits the organisation, but fails to fit the job. This causes the applicant to be rejected.

12

Reject this person

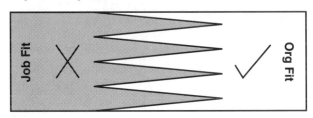

In the third picture, the applicant fits the job, but fails to fit the organisation. This also causes the applicant to be rejected.

Reject this person

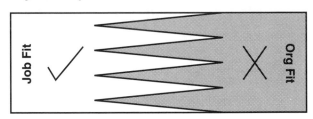

SUMMARY – CHAPTER 1

- Organisational entry is the whole process of finding a new member of staff. It begins when you sense you need to recruit someone and ends when the newcomer is settled and effective.

- Recruitment is the process of attracting suitably qualified people to apply for the position.

- Selection is the process of assessing applicants and choosing whom to employ.

- Introduction is the process of helping the newcomer survive their first day at work.

- The traditional approach to recruitment and selection is incomplete for a number of reasons:
  - job analyses quickly become dated
  - employees change jobs and organisations
  - it is only concerned with finding new recruits
  - introduction and socialisation are often forgotten
  - it only considers the organisation's needs
  - it doesn't mirror actual practice.

- A new approach to organisational entry considers how applicants fit the job and how they fit into the organisation.

13

2
■ ■ ■
How do you select fairly?

CHAPTER OBJECTIVES

After reading this chapter, you should:
- know what the law says about organisational entry
- understand what constitutes unfair discrimination
- be able to identify unfairness in recruitment and selection
- be able to avoid adopting unfair methods when recruiting.

CHAPTER OVERVIEW

The legal aspects of organisational entry concern many managers. Legal considerations are commonly seen as perplexing and the mysterious preserve of highly trained and highly priced solicitors. Ignorance of the law can translate itself into several types of behaviour during selection. The manager who steers clear of any potentially controversial area, and the manager who just ignores all legal considerations are both common manifestations of the problem. Both forms of behaviour reduce the effectiveness of the organisational entry system and may make the manager legally liable. In reality, managers need not fear the law. The law relating to organisational entry is quite straightforward and easy to understand. In this chapter, I hope to allay your fears and show you that an understanding of the laws relating to organisational entry is essential because it can actually help you become a more effective recruiter. I shall outline the key laws, and look at some ways that you can avoid contravening them.

What is discrimination?
■ ■ ■

Discrimination is at the heart of selection. You need to discriminate between candidates to identify who will be the most effective employee. But at the same time, you need to discriminate fairly. There are three reasons why you should discriminate fairly:

- there are legal considerations which must be obeyed
- it is ethically and morally more acceptable
- you will maximise the performance of your team and your organisation.

This last point is essential. Even if there were no laws governing how we discriminate, we would still want to discriminate fairly and give every applicant an equal chance to prove themselves. At the heart of good organisational entry is a set of selection criteria which clearly lays out the standards by which applicants should be judged. By sticking to this, you maximise the likelihood that you will recruit the most effective new employee. If you move away from the selection criteria and discriminate unfairly, you are more likely to recruit someone less able, which is to no one's advantage.

15

What does the law say?
■ ■ ■

It is unlawful to discriminate against people at any stage in the recruitment and selection process for the following reasons:

- their gender
- their race, nationality or ethnic or national origins
- because they are married.

It is *not* unlawful, but usually unwise, to discriminate against people because of their age, the fact they are single, their sexual orientation, attractiveness, disabilities, religious or political beliefs (except in Northern Ireland where racial discrimination legislation does not apply), social class, appearance, mannerisms, schooling and education, residence and so on. However, there is other legislation, which must be taken into consideration, relating to:

- people with disabilities
- young people, children and women
- foreign nationals
- ex-offenders.

While it may not be unlawful to discriminate against these categories of people, most people, myself included, believe that it is morally wrong to discriminate in this way. It is also dysfunctional for the organisation as you are unlikely to select the most effective person for the job.

The law in Britain is under increasing pressure from European legislation. There have been challenges recently to the European Court of Justice on several employment law issues, such as the Armed Services' dismissal of pregnant women. These decisions have jurisdiction over the British courts and create binding obligations on Britain. In addition, decisions taken by the European Court of Human Rights are, by convention, converted into British law, even though it does not have jurisdiction over British courts. On mainland Europe, just as in Britain, there is an increasing acknowledgement that discrimination on the grounds of age, sexual orientation, disability and the like is morally unacceptable. Many people suspect that, in time, this will result in appeals to the European courts and the definition of unfair discrimination will be broadened. This might begin with the issue of the right to privacy.

16

Every citizen of a European Union country has the right to be treated equally and has a right to privacy. So enquiries during organisational entry into a person's private life might be deemed to contravene European law. Further, the European Court judgements have been retrospective, i.e. the decision dates back to the time when the member country began breaking the Treaty of Rome, and therefore, any future findings may be similarly backdated. So, discrimination on the grounds of sexual orientation, age, religious belief and so on, which might be deemed to contravene the Treaty of Rome in the future, would seem to be particularly unwise.

Types of discrimination

Discrimination falls into three categories:

- **Direct discrimination** – occurs where candidates are treated less favourably because of their gender, race or marital status. An example is the following advertisement 'Men needed for road sweeping duties'. Direct discrimination is also known as 'disparate treatment'.

- **Indirect discrimination** – occurs where a condition set by a recruiter, such as a height requirement (on average women are shorter than men), cannot be met equally by people of different genders, races, or marital status. A condition might be thought to be fair because it is universally applied to all applicants; this is not so. If the effect of the condition produces unfair results, then indirect discrimination has taken place. The courts have held that indirect discrimination must be an *absolute bar* to getting the job for it to be unlawful. Indirect discrimination is also known as 'adverse impact'.

■ **Victimisation** – occurs where people are treated less favourably because they have used or have alleged contravention of the legislation.

Discrimination on the grounds of gender

There are two pieces of legislation that are usually referred to:

■ Sex Discrimination Act 1975
■ Equal Pay Act 1970.

The Sex Discrimination Act 1975 (SDA) states that is unlawful to discriminate on the grounds of someone's gender. This refers to discrimination against both men and women. The Sex Discrimination Act also prevents employers discriminating against someone because they are married, but not against single people. The Equal Pay Act 1970 states that it is unlawful to pay men and women differently if their work is either:

■ broadly similar in nature
■ rated as equivalent
■ of equal value.

The Equal Pay Act only comes into operation after the newcomer has joined the organisation, as it is related to contractual equality. However, selectors would be wise to take account of it during the organisational entry process to avoid future problems.

Despite the major changes in society over the past twenty or thirty years, many managers are still unaware of their own discriminatory behaviour. The following questions illustrate how difficult it can be to discriminate fairly.

What is a fair question?

Would the following questions be fair if asked at an interview?
● Do you have any children?
● How will your partner react if you have to spend nights away from home?
● What would you say to a female member of staff who said that she didn't like having a male boss?

All these questions are unlawful and unfair. The first question is clearly unfair because it is not job related, but it is also unlawful, because even if it is asked of every applicant, the answers from men and women are likely to be interpreted differently. Unreasonable, but stereotypical, responses might be that men with children are solid and committed to their responsibilities, whereas women with children are likely to take more time off work. The second question is similarly unfair and unlawful because it might be answered differently by men and women. Men are likely to be disadvantaged by the third question because it doesn't apply to women.

Discrimination on the grounds of race

The Race Relations Act 1976 (RRA) prohibits discrimination on the grounds of race. The Act defines race in terms of race, colour, nationality, or ethnic or national origins. Religious discrimination is not outlawed, except in Northern Ireland, but the courts have held that Sikhs and Rastafarians are racial groups. Both the RRA and the SDA apply to the promotion and transfer of all staff as well as to the recruitment and selection of applicants from outside the organisation.

18

Circumstances where sex and race discrimination are lawful

There are circumstances where sex and race discrimination are lawful. This occurs when being of a particular sex or race is a genuine occupational qualification (GOQ). The courts have been very reluctant to suspend the SDA and RRA and grant a job GOQ status. The following circumstances have been held to be a GOQ:

- reasons of authenticity in a dramatic performance, or other entertainment
- for reasons of physiology *other* than for physical strength or stamina
- to preserve decency or privacy, although this is only reluctantly awarded. (In one case, an employer claimed that only men were required to work in a men's clothing shop. However, the Industrial Tribunal rejected this as there were changing rooms available for customers and other male employees could take inside leg measurements and the like.)
- where the employee must live on the premises and the premises only have sleeping accommodation and sanitary facilities for one sex and it is not reasonable to expect the organisation to make the necessary changes or supply alternative accommodation

- in a hospital, prison or similar establishment where the people looked after are of the same sex and require special care, attention or supervision
- when the employee is promoting educational or welfare personal services that make gender or race relevant
- when the job includes overseas duties that could not be done because the other country's laws or customs prohibit men, women or certain races from doing the work
- if a job is one of two, the husband or wife can be discriminated against if their partner holds the other job.

If you are unsure whether a job is covered by one of the above, you should contact either the Equal Opportunities Commission or the Commission for Racial Equality for free advice beforehand. You can find the addresses at the back of this book.

People with disabilities

19

The Disabled Persons (Employment) Act 1944 (DPA) states that organisations of twenty or more employees (government departments and NHS excluded) have a duty to ensure that usually 3% or more of their workforce are people with disabilities. It is not an offence to be under the quota, but the organisation has a duty to recruit only people with disabilities until the quota is met. If there are no suitable registered disabled people available, then you can apply to the Department of Employment for a permit to employ someone who is not registered disabled. In practice, however, the Department of Employment has issued blanket permits to many organisations exempting them from the quota provided that they consider sympathetically any applications from people with disabilities.

The ineffectiveness of the employment legislation concerning people with disabilities has led to many calls for it to be repealed and new legislation that will give people with disabilities full protection introduced. This happened towards the end of 1995 with the Royal Assent of The Disability Act 1995. This act repeals the current quota scheme and confers protection to people with disabilities similar to that which the SDA and RRA give to all men, women and racial groups. In short, it means that discrimination against people with disabilities is now legally regarded as being broadly similar to sex or race discrimination. The act comes into force towards the end of 1996.

The Disability Act 1995 applies to organisations employing twenty people or more and has four main provisions:

- to qualify a person must have, or have had, a physical or mental impairment that is causing a substantial and long term adverse effect on their abilities to carry out normal day-to-day duties
- it is unlawful to treat a person less favourably, for a reason related to their past or present disability, than a person to whom that reason does not, or would not apply
- it is unlawful for an employer to treat a disabled person less favourably, unless there is good reason which is substantial and material to the particular case
- an employer is obliged to make reasonable adjustments to premises and conditions to prevent disadvantage occurring including:
  - giving some duties to other employees
  - changing working hours
  - changing the location of the job
  - acquiring or modifying equipment
  - arranging leave for rehabilitation or treatment
  - organising supervision
  - providing a reader or interpreter.

20

Two types of job are reserved for people with disabilities:

- car park attendants
- lift attendants.

People in these jobs do not count towards the organisation's quota.

Fortunately, most people don't know what it is like to be barred from a job because they have a serious disability. This ignorance can lead to bewilderment about the necessity of having legislation to protect people with disabilities.

What is it like to have a disability?

For this activity you will need about half an hour, a friend or colleague that you can trust, and a blindfold. Take it in turns to wear the blindfold for about fifteen minutes each. Make sure that it is absolutely pitch black when you are wearing it. Then, with your friend or colleague as a guide, go for a walk. The guide should not touch you and is only there to ensure that you don't come to any harm. The guide should avoid roads and make sure that you don't walk into anything especially at knee, crotch or eye level. Once you've both had a go, try answering the following questions:

- what did it feel like to be blindfolded?
- what senses did you use?
- how did you change as a person when you were blindfolded?

The purpose of this activity is to raise your awareness of equal opportunity issues. The majority of managers in Britain are middle class, white men (as am I). Consequently, it is middle class, white men who do most of the recruiting for organisations. Equal opportunities policies are often mockingly 'put down' by managers who can't see the relevance of the legislation. And why should they? They have probably never been discriminated against because of their gender, race, colour or disability.

When wearing the blindfold, most people find that their senses are improved rather than lessened. People start to recognise others by smell, they sense open space and junctions in the corridor by the feel of the air on their skin, and they hear so much more. But the point of this activity is not to demonstrate how your other senses develop to compensate for your loss of sight. It is to highlight the real nature of disabilities. Your eyes were not functioning. You were still the same person with the same needs and wants, the same objectives, the same likes and dislikes, the same friends and enemies. In short, you were exactly the same person. You simply couldn't see.

21

Young people, children and women

The Children and Young Persons Act 1933 (CYPA) and the Children and Young Persons Act 1937 state that it is unlawful to employ children below the age of 13. This includes working without pay if the job is carried out for profit. The CYPA also says that a child must not lift, carry or move anything heavy that is likely to cause them injury. It is unlawful to employ any child below the minimum school-leaving age during school hours, and it is unlawful to employ such a child before 7 am or after 7 pm on any day. Anyone aged under 18 is prohibited from working in places where alcohol is sold and consumed and in betting shops. No one under the age of 18 is bound by a contract of employment unless the contract is, on the whole, beneficial to them. However, such a contract is binding upon the employer.

Women are prohibited by the Employment Act 1989 from working in certain lead manufacturing processes and from working in a factory within four weeks of giving birth. There are also some restrictions preventing women from working under the Ionising Radiations Regulations.

Foreign nationals

You are allowed to ask applicants for proof that they can work in the UK. Generally, work permits are required by non-European Union citizens. These are obtained from the Department of Employment and usually take more than eight weeks to process. They are needed before the person can begin work and you need proof of the applicant's skills, qualifications and abilities. Work permits are issued when you can prove that the vacancy cannot be filled by a European Union citizen. As a result, they are usually only issued to highly skilled and/or professional workers.

Ex-offenders

The Rehabilitation of Offenders Act 1974 states that ex-offenders do not have to reveal their 'spent' convictions if the sentence has been served. It also says that you may not discriminate against ex-offenders if you have knowledge of such 'spent' convictions and that ex-offenders are allowed to deny that they have such a criminal record. A conviction is said to be 'spent' if the rehabilitation period has elapsed without further offence. Rehabilitation periods vary as follows:

Conviction	Rehabilitation Period
Imprisonment over 30 months	Lifetime
Imprisonment between 6 and 30 months	10 years
Imprisonment less than 6 months	7 years
Probation order, conditional discharge or binding over	1 year (or until the order expires)
Absolute discharges	6 months

There are exceptions to this right to silence. Applicants for some jobs must declare all previous convictions. These include:

- doctors, midwives, nurses, dentists and veterinary surgeons
- pharmacists and opticians
- teachers
- social workers and probation officers
- barristers and solicitors
- accountants
- police constables
- people with access to minors or patients.

Applicants for these jobs must reveal all convictions, 'spent' or not, and can be denied employment because of the conviction. Applicants for any other job do not have to disclose voluntarily spent or unspent convictions. As a result, you are advised to inquire about applicants' previous convictions if you are concerned.

Positive discrimination and positive action

The law relating to sex and race discrimination relates to men and women and to black and white alike. It is as unfair to discriminate against the majority as it is to discriminate against the minority. Consequently, positive discrimination (the favouring of less meritorious applicants from an under-represented group to improve representation of the group) is unlawful.

Positive action, on the other hand, is perfectly legal. Positive action is the encouragement of people from under-represented groups to apply for the position. So, you are allowed to place advertisements for jobs in publications likely to be read by the under-represented group, or you might say something like the following in the advertisement, 'We encourage applications from people with disabilities'. However, you are not allowed to select (i.e. choose between candidates) on these grounds, nor are you allowed to place your job advertisements only in selected publications that are likely to exclude certain groups of people, such as *Penthouse* or *Mayfair* (predominantly male readership), or *Gay News* (predominantly gay and lesbian readership). While positive action is tolerated, selection between candidates must be on merit.

23

Summary

So far in this chapter, I have discussed what the law says in connection with recruitment and selection in the UK. Unfortunately, the law is rather ineffective in preventing discriminatory practice. However, I would argue that it is essential that you recruit fairly as this will help you find the person who will perform most effectively. By judging applicants with reference to selection criteria, you will recruit the person who will contribute most positively to performance.

Developments in the USA

It is often said that we in Britain follow managerial developments in the USA. There certainly seems to be some truth in this with regard to equal opportunities policy. For example, sex and race discrimination legislation first appeared in America in the mid-1960s when Congress passed the Civil Rights Act – a decade earlier than in the UK. Currently there is a discrepancy between the two countries in the ways in which discrimination is adjudged. In Britain, we seem much less stringent and much less rigorous than in the States. In the States, for example, organisations must show that selection tests have content, criterion and construct validity and they must also be reliable.

- Content validity – the selection tests measure a representative sample of the skills, behaviour etc. related to job performance.
- Criterion validity – the scores obtained from selection tests are related to job performance.
- Construct validity – the selection tests must measure what they are supposed to measure.
- Reliability – the tests produce the same results regardless of the person conducting the test, do so consistently for all applicants, and yield the same results if applicants are tested again.

If a test has validity on all four counts you can be fairly confident that you have a fair test. A series of US court decisions has made it the responsibility of the organisation to check that its selection tests are valid on these four counts. This is usually achieved through statistical analysis.

In Britain, the courts so far have preferred a more qualitative position. However, if we continue to follow where the American courts lead, selectors will soon have to be more rigorous in ensuring that the tests they use are fair. It would be wise, and ethically correct, to pre-empt any new developments in this field by ensuring now that your selection tests are valid for content, criterion and construct and are reliable. This will help you make better selection decisions, if nothing else.

Now that I have examined the legislation affecting recruitment and selection practice in the UK, I will discuss how you can avoid contravening the law. The rest of the chapter concentrates on this practical issue.

Avoiding unfairness

■ ■ ■

Make objective decisions

The key to making fair selection decisions is objectivity. Your decisions at every stage of the process should result from reasoned analysis, uninfluenced by emotion, impulse or prejudice. This is easier said than done, as it is easy to convince ourselves that we are being objective when we are not.

'I really liked Amanda and I was impressed with her commitment. She's obviously got what it takes to get sales. All that energy and enthusiasm. She'll pick up the job quickly and she'll fit in so well with everyone.'

'Yes, it's a pity that Kevin was so quiet. He's got all the skills and a good track record in the industry. But, can you see him surviving in the team?'

'Shame though. But yes, I agree, it has to be Amanda.'

This short example, typical of so many decisions, illustrates how easy it is to make spurious choices. Kevin has the proven skills and the experience to succeed in the job, whereas Amanda is untried and untested in the role. The interviewers favour Amanda because they like her and then find specious reasons to justify their decision. However, if you were to talk to these interviewers they would almost certainly believe that they had chosen fairly.

This illustrates the importance of setting out your selection criteria well before you meet the candidates. You then use these criteria when gathering information during the selection tests. Had the criteria in this instance included items related to organisation fit, then questioning about this issue would have yielded evidence to help the selectors make a decision. For example, candidates could have been asked to relate examples of how working with other people had helped them achieve their objectives. In this way, Kevin's potential fit to the team could have been investigated and information gathered so that an informed objective decision could be made rather than guessed at. In the example, a subjective decision of his fit was used to create negative 'evidence' with which to weaken his case in favour of a 'preferred' applicant.

Obtain evidence to support your decisions

You should have evidence relating to the selection criteria to support every selection decision you make. If you do not, then you will make subjective decisions. One way to ensure objectivity is to imagine justifying your decisions to an independent person using the selection criteria. This reveals whether or not the reasons for your choices are related to your original analysis of the job and the organisation.

Unfair discrimination can appear at any part of the organisational entry process. It is not just confined to 'dodgy' questions in an interview or subjective choices. Detailed discussion of unfair discrimination is an integral part of the chapters that deal with the analysis, recruitment, and selection stages of organisational entry.

> Imagine that you have to justify your selection
> decisions (using the selection criteria) to an
> independent person.

Be systematic

Being systematic helps to ensure that you don't get diverted from your goal of making fair and objective decisions. It is all too easy, for example, when filtering a large batch of CVs to forget the selection criteria. By systematically setting out your criteria at every stage, you increase the chances of making fair and good decisions.

Being systematic is also the minimum safeguard that any tribunal or court would expect. If you have not adopted a systematic process, then you will have great difficulty defending yourself against any accusations of discriminatory behaviour.

26

Identifying unfairness
■ ■ ■

Look around at work. Is there a representative mix of different types of people from the local community at all levels in the organisation? Probably not. Unfortunately, there is very little you can do about the existing balance. Your task when recruiting new members of staff is to ensure that you give every applicant an equal chance to measure themselves against the selection criteria. But how do you identify whether or not you have been fair?

The most important thing to do is keep accurate and timely records that monitor all characteristics of applicants that you are interested in at every stage of the process. Analysis of these records reveals whether or not the selection techniques you have used have been fair to under-represented groups. The initial pool of candidates should be broadly representative of the community, although this might be moderated by any positive action strategies that you have used, and this should be replicated at every subsequent stage of the process. This is not always easy to monitor because the filtering of applicants to smaller, more manageable, numbers means that you will rarely have a large enough pool of applicants to produce statistically significant figures. However, you should be able to analyse the initial pool of applicants, the mix of those shortlisted and, probably, those chosen from the first selection stage. The following table will help you analyse whether or not any part of your organisational entry process discriminates unfairly.

This table contains a typical choice of races that organisations often seek to monitor. Of course, you would need to adapt this to suit your particular needs, and you must do the same to monitor the mix of men and women at every stage. You can use a similar table to analyse any under-represented group that you wish to monitor. You might, for example, want to monitor how the organisational entry process discriminates in favour of, or against, younger applicants.

	Community	Attraction	Shortlist	Selection 1	Selection 2	Selection 3
Black – African						
Black – Caribbean						
Black – Other						
Indian						
Pakistani						
Bangladeshi						
Chinese						
White – UK/Irish						
White – European						
Other						

27

The column headed 'community' contains the population mix of the community from which you want to recruit. A trip to the library or a call to the council should get you a breakdown of the racial mix of your community. If you are advertising the post fairly, you should attract a mix of races similar to the mix in the community. If you are selecting fairly, the mix should remain fairly constant throughout the organisational entry process.

Be careful of changes of mix that cancel themselves out during the process. These might indicate that different aspects of the process are unfair and that chance has neutralised the imbalance. In all likelihood, these contrasting effects will not neutralise the unfairness. Instead, bad decisions will probably have been made at more than one stage of the process, causing good applicants to be rejected.

By analysing your organisational entry process in this way, you will get an indication of whether or not you have been unfair and, if you have, where in the process the unfairness has occurred. This is a vital control mechanism for the identification of unfairness. When you come to recruit again, you will know the potential pitfalls that might recur and you can take steps to avoid them happening again.

SUMMARY – CHAPTER 2

- There are three reasons why you must discriminate fairly:
  – to abide by the law
  – ethical and moral reasons
  – to find the most effective person.

- It is unlawful to discriminate against someone because of their gender, race or because they are married.

- There are three types of discrimination:
  – direct discrimination
  – indirect discrimination
  – victimisation.

- To avoid being unfair you should ensure that you:
  – make objective decisions
  – obtain evidence to support your decisions
  – are systematic.

- To check whether you are being fair, you should monitor the mix of applicants of every stage of the organisational entry process.

28

3
■ ■ ■

How do you make a sensible decision?

CHAPTER OVERVIEW

Organisational entry is a decision making process. So, this chapter begins by looking at decision making in general, before transferring a rational model to organisational entry. The organisational entry process is then broken down into nine stages, which form the backbone of the book. By working through the nine stages, you will obtain the knowledge you need to recruit effectively. The remaining chapters in the book concentrate sequentially on each stage in the process.

What is a rational decision?
■ ■ ■

Organisational entry is a decision making process. At the start of this book, I suggested that it is often the biggest and most important decision that managers must make. It is a decision that needs to be carefully and systematically considered. You want to find the person most likely to perform well. The person you recruit wants to find satisfying, rewarding and challenging work. The best way to ensure that this happens is to adopt a rational approach.

Rational decision making has several stages. In a basic form, it can be broken down to six:

> ### THE 6 STAGES OF THE RATIONAL DECISION MAKING PROCESS
>
> 1 *Sense* that you have a problem
> 2 *Define* the nature of the problem
> 3 *Specify* your objectives and criteria
> 4 *Generate* possible solutions
> 5 *Evaluate* each of the options against the criteria
> 6 *Choose* the best solution

This model for solving problems or making decisions is integral to much management theory and applicable to a very wide range of topics. You must first sense that you have a problem, which you then analyse to understand its nature and the sort of solution that might be acceptable. Having analysed the problem, you outline your objectives or criteria before looking for ways to solve it. You then generate a range of possible solutions or options. These are compared against your criteria and the best fit is chosen. By adopting a decision strategy, such as the one outlined, you avoid the problems of jumping to conclusions and investigate a range of solutions, rather than having pre-set ideas about what is required.

But there are potential problems with such a strategy. Possibly the most important one to recognise is that it is a sequential strategy, i.e. a process where each stage follows the previous one. The danger with this is that mistakes made at one stage cascade down through the whole process. The earlier stages, especially the analysis, are vital, as these dictate the shape of future events. More than this though, the whole process can take on a momentum of its own with good or bad practice early on continuing through all the later stages.

Organisational entry as a rational decision
■ ■ ■

How does the six stage model of rational decision making map on to organisational entry? Let's take it one stage at a time.

Stage 1: Sense that you have a problem

In the introduction, I related the story of Pascale and Rob. In that story, Pascale realised she had a problem the moment John resigned. It didn't need great deductive powers to establish the fact. Unfortunately, it's not always so obvious that you need to recruit someone.

Ann is the manager of a new business department in a credit card company. Her staff receive completed application forms from potential customers and key them into the computer system. The computer automatically credit scores them and produces acceptance or rejection letters. In addition, if a customer is accepted the computer generates the necessary commands for the printing of the customer's credit card and associated mail. The printing of blank cards happens in a secure room with limited access. All of these functions are managed by Ann and she has forty staff in her department. These break down in the following way: thirty staff keying-in application forms with three supervisors; and, six staff in the secure room with one supervisor.

The department begins work at eight in the morning and ends at six in the evening with staff on a form of flexitime. New promotional campaigns have seen a rise in the number of applications being received, and campaigns are planned that are estimated to increase the number of application forms the department receives over the next six months by 30%. What should Ann do?

31

Is this a time for recruiting a new person, or people, or not? From the information to hand it is impossible to tell, but Ann seems to have several possibilities. She could:

- take on more staff on permanent contracts on the assumption that either the increased activity will continue or natural wastage will take care of the extra staff in six months time
- take on staff on short term contracts to cope with the excess
- take on temporary staff on a daily, weekly or monthly basis
- look to see if there are staff in other departments who might lend a hand with the excess
- extend the working hours and offer overtime
- adopt a combination of some or all of these measures
- do nothing and build up a backlog.

How do you solve a problem like this? As with the complete organisational entry system, the rational decision making model can be of considerable advantage. Had Ann used it, she would have generated as many options as possible and then tried to evaluate each one and every combination. Unfortunately, even using a rational approach there might be many unanswered questions. How accurate are the forecasts of more applications likely to be? How will staff respond to working longer hours? Can appropriately skilled people be found? How long are the learning curves for new staff?

The purpose of relating this example is to demonstrate that it isn't always obvious when you need to recruit someone. The only solution is to use your managerial judgement to determine the best course of action. But one thing remains constant: there are always options.

> 1 **Managerial judgement is always needed to determine whether new employees are necessary.**
> 2 **There are always alternatives to recruiting new employees.**

Stage 2: Define the nature of the problem

Once you've decided that you need to recruit a new member of staff, the next stage is to think through the implications of your decision. In particular, you need to think about three things:

- how your decision to recruit someone fits in with the organisation's policies and strategies
- how the newcomer will affect existing employees and working practices
- how you will go about finding someone and introducing them to their work.

Stage 3: Specify your objectives and criteria

This is the analysis stage of the process. Traditionally, the focus at this stage is on the job and the knowledge, skills, abilities and other characteristics required to perform well. A wise manager would think about the environment in which the new employee will be working, and the characteristics needed to thrive in it. And, of course, you need to analyse the organisational requirements mentioned in stage 2.

The findings of your analysis indicate the type of qualities you want to find. These qualities divide into:

- **essential criteria** – applicants must satisfy these to be considered as possible recruits
- **desirable criteria** – mainly used to differentiate between applicants.

The criteria are important because they are at the heart of the rational approach to decision making. If you make a mistake with your 'selection criteria', you are unlikely to find the best person.

Stage 4: Generate possible solutions

Looking at organisational entry rationally, the possible solutions are people. So, the generation of possible solutions refers to the stage of the process where you attract people to apply for the job. This stage was defined earlier as recruitment.

Stage 5: Evaluate the options against the criteria

Having generated a number of possible solutions you now need to evaluate each one against the criteria you specified earlier in the process. Comparing people to the criteria occurs at various stages. The most common are the filtering of CVs and application forms, the assessment of references, and the decision at the end of an interview. This activity was defined earlier as selection.

Stage 6: Choose the best solution

This stage is self-explanatory. The idea is that the person most closely aligned to the selection criteria is the person offered the job.

What are the stages of organisational entry?
■ ■ ■

Mapping the organisational entry process on to a model of rational decision making is important because it highlights the key aspects of the process, i.e. analysis, establishing selection criteria, and comparing applicants to the selection criteria. This skeleton lies beneath all systematic organisational entry processes and is the foundation for fair, efficient and effective organisational entry.

The rational model has several limitations that need further discussion. First, it concentrates on the initial stages of the process and fails to differentiate or include some of the processes special to organisational entry. Second, it focuses solely on the selection decision and does not include other important issues such as the integration of the newcomer in the organisation. Third, it is only concerned with the decision from the organisation's perspective and fails to acknowledge that applicants make decisions too. These limitations mean that whilst the rational model is useful for outlining the key processes in organisational entry, it needs to be reframed for use when finding a new member of staff.

The organisational entry process has nine main components which handily (with a bit of manipulation) all begin with the letter A; hence the title of the '9A Organisational Entry Cycle'.

THE 9A ORGANISATIONAL ENTRY CYCLE

1 Approach (design a recruitment strategy)
2 Analysis (job and organisational analysis)
3 Attraction (interest a pool of candidates)
4 Assessment (choose the 'best' candidate)
5 Agreement (negotiate the deal)
6 Adjustment (help the newcomer manage stress)
7 Adaptation (help the newcomer adapt)
8 Attrition (keep good people)
9 Audit (check the system has worked effectively)

34

Each of these components can be broken down further into a series of subprocesses.

Approach

Before you can embark on an organisational entry campaign, you need to think through your strategy. What are you trying to achieve? What are your objectives? How does your recruitment fit in with the human resource and business strategy of the organisation? What competencies is your organisation keen to acquire?

In addition, you need to think about the shape of your organisational entry strategy. Who has to be involved? What alternatives are there? What is your time scale? What does your organisation expect of you? Too often, managers jump in and place advertisements before they have thought what it is they want to achieve. In the next chapter, I shall take you through the various things you should be considering before you start doing anything.

Analysis

The rational decision making model highlights the analysis stage of the organisational entry process. Any mistakes made at this stage tend to cascade down through the rest of the process and are likely to lead to you not recruiting the best person for the job. There are several factors that you need to analyse:

- your current and, as far as possible, future staffing needs
- the nature of the job newcomers will do
- the organisation's culture
- how a newcomer will change and affect existing employees and patterns of work.

The purpose of the analysis is to understand exactly the sort of person you need: what are the critical factors leading to high performance? Also, what sort of person will get satisfaction from the work? This analysis is then used to put together the criteria for accepting or rejecting candidates in the selection phase of the process. I will show you how to construct selection criteria in chapter 5.

Attraction

The attraction phase, also called recruitment, refers specifically to the process of interesting suitable candidates. This will involve you in the choice of appropriate methods for locating, finding, and communicating with possible applicants, designing advertisements, managing the work of consultants, and all the associated administration of the process. I shall cover each of these topics in chapter 6.

Assessment

The selection stage is often viewed as being the most difficult and most important stage to do well. I would strongly dispute this. If you have properly analysed your requirements and produced a suitable and realistic set of selection criteria – *and you are truly prepared to make choices based on the selection criteria* – then selection becomes a relatively straightforward task. It is simply learning a number of skills and techniques for extracting the information you want from applicants and applying those skills and techniques in an appropriate manner. These subjects are covered in chapter 7.

Agreement

There is another set of factors that you must bear in mind when choosing whom to select. These factors concern the manner of selection and the effect this has on subsequent employee performance. In particular, the manner of selection affects the formation of the psychological contract between the newcomer and the organisation. Viewed in this way, selection is not simply a hurdle that must be cleared by the applicant to gain entry into the organisation, it is part of the relationship between the two parties that has a significant impact in shaping the expectations of each about the other. It plays a major role in determining the atmosphere of the relationship which, in turn, affects subsequent performance and levels of satisfaction. Forming the psychological contract is a vital part of any organisational entry exercise. This important topic is covered in chapter 8.

What has shaped your relationship with your employer?

To illustrate this point, think back over your relationship with your employer. To what extent do you recall your selection experience? How has it shaped your relationship with the organisation? What expectations did you have when you started and how have these changed?

Adjustment

Introduction is possibly the most frequently ignored aspect of organisational entry. Much time and money is spent finding and choosing suitable new staff, but relatively little is spent helping to integrate the newcomer into the organisation or new job. Once an offer is accepted, many recruiters appear to think that the whole process is completed. Nothing could be further from the truth. Starting a new job is one of the most stressful times in a person's career. Chapter 9 examines what you can do to ease the newcomer into their new job so that you minimise the stress of the role transition and help them become effective as quickly as possible. This needs to take place on the first day of employment, if not before.

Adaptation

The early moments of a person's relationship with an organisation are rather like the formative years of childhood. The unusual and different loom large and fascinate, the strange intrigues, and the unpleasant causes alarm and hostile reaction. So, once the newcomer has got over the initial stress of changing jobs, their attention shifts. They now have to make sense of the new and strange things happening around them. It is a time of dramatic change and adaptation, a time when the people in an organisation need to be particularly sensitive to the needs of newcomers. In chapter 10, I shall introduce you to several techniques that you can use to help newcomers integrate into your organisation. These include buddying and mentoring.

Attrition

After you have invested all that time, effort and money in finding an excellent new employee and then doubled your investment by providing training, how can you make sure that the person doesn't leave?

There are many ways to tackle this question, but I shall concentrate on the topic of career management in chapter 11.

Audit

The concept of the control loop is one of the most fundamental of all management ideas. Put simply, a control loop is a method of checking whether you have achieved what you wanted to achieve. If you have not, then corrective action has to be taken. The control loop is an essential part of organisational entry, especially if you recruit new staff regularly.

Imagine that you are about to recruit for the second time. What would you do first? One option is to begin by assessing your needs. Another option is to look back at the previous organisational entry episode and see what can be learnt from that experience. Did it yield someone who could do the job well? Has the newcomer settled in well? Is their performance at the level that you expected?

Whatever your answers to these questions, they give you valuable information about the effectiveness of your organisational entry practice. For example, if it went wrong, you can use that knowledge to help ensure that it doesn't go wrong again. In chapter 12, I develop these ideas and show you how you can learn from your own previous experience of organisational entry.

Vicious and virtuous circles

In this chapter, I've described a rational process to help you find a new member of staff. By describing such a process, I have implied that if you follow it through you will find the best person for the job. Unfortunately, it isn't that simple. You have to want to be effective and give organisational entry its due. A manager who's 'switched on' to the importance and gravity of the situation is much more likely to invest time and effort, and to tackle the mental issue of confronting their own prejudice, than someone who is not so committed – even if they adopt the process described in this chapter.

Think back to the case study in the introduction. In that example Pascale set a vicious circle in motion when she recruited Juliet because she hadn't realised the importance or gravity of the situation. A vicious circle is a chain of events that compound each other. As one thing goes wrong, then the next thing goes wrong and so on. In this case, the decision to recruit someone without properly assessing the person led to an ill-advised decision, which led to the newcomer performing poorly, which is likely to lead to poor performance and Pascale being viewed as a manager who can't run her department effectively.

Imagine if she had properly prepared her organisational entry strategy and had asked questions that revealed the best candidate. Then by comparing all applicants to the selection criteria she would have been more likely to find a suitable new employee. The newcomer would be effective, their efficiency would rub off on Pascale and she would be viewed as a manager running an efficient and effective department. She would have created a virtuous circle.

The point of relating this story is simple: you have to give organisational entry its due, and you have to want to make the right decision if you are to find the right person. Knowing what to do isn't sufficient.

> **You must want to find the right person: give organisational entry its due!**

SUMMARY - CHAPTER 3

- A rational approach to making a decision has six stages:
  - sense that you have a problem
  - define the nature of the problem
  - specify your objectives and criteria
  - generate possible solutions
  - evaluate the options against the criteria
  - choose the best solution.

- Organisational entry should be a rational decision.

- Organisational entry has nine stages:
  - approach (design a strategy)
  - analysis (of job and organisation)
  - attraction (interest a pool of candidates)
  - assessment (choose the best fit)
  - agreement (negotiate the deal)
  - adjustment (manage the stress of the first day)
  - adaption (help the newcomer adapt)
  - attrition (keep good people)
  - audit (check it all worked).

- Recruiting the right person starts a virtuous circle.

- Recruiting the wrong person starts a vicious circle.

- You must *want* to find the right person: give organisational entry its due.

4

· · ·

What does your organisation require of you?

CHAPTER OBJECTIVES

After reading this chapter, you should be able to:
- gather information about the organisational entry requirements that your organisation has of you
- analyse the staffing needs of your team
- analyse the mix of competencies in your team
- assess whether there is a need to look outside the organisation or team for new staff
- conduct a cost benefit analysis of your organisational entry process
- explain why it is important to invest in organisational entry.

CHAPTER OVERVIEW

In this chapter, I look at a preliminary activity that must be carried out before the search for a new member of staff can begin. This activity is an assessment of the needs of your organisation. Do you really need to recruit someone? What competencies are required? What systems and procedures must you abide by? And finally, what are the cost benefits of being thorough with organisational entry?

What are your staffing requirements?
■ ■ ■

In the late 1980s and 1990s, 'hire 'em, fire 'em' staffing strategies became ubiquitous in British industry. Employers, unsure of the economic climate, wanted to remain flexible so that they could react to changes in the environment. In hindsight, many employers now see the costs arising from 'hire 'em, fire 'em' staffing strategies. These include:

- recruitment
- training
- redundancy and outplacement packages and disruption
- costs related to the learning curve of new employees
- more managerial time spent on managing employee related issues
- a workforce more concerned with its own development and interests than those of the organisation.

There are many other costs. The 'hire 'em, fire 'em' strategies also tend to produce an anxious managerial team worried whether one mistake might cause their dismissal. This is a short term strategy that reduces the likelihood of risk taking, creativity, and innovation appearing. Advocates would say that it keeps everyone on their toes and ensures that there is no slack in the system. Others, myself included, would say that this is a short-sighted, callous way to treat people that is, ultimately, dysfunctional for the organisation.

Interestingly, there are examples of many organisations keen not to be identified with such strategies. Instead, they believe that the organisation's relationship with employees needs to be long term, with each party committed to the success of the other. For example, Rover now gives all employees a substantial sum of money every year to spend on any educational programme they want. One London firm of solicitors pays for, and arranges, French lessons for its staff. Employee share option schemes and the like similarly help to integrate employer and employee interests.

However, no matter how strongly one advocates longer term staffing strategies in preference to 'hire 'em, fire 'em' strategies, organisations need to be competitive and, in most cases, staff related costs are a major expenditure affecting profitability. Organisations need to be the right size to pursue their objectives. Rather than adopt 'rightsizing', a fashionable euphemism for disposing of unwanted staff, it is preferable to recruit new staff only when you are sure that they will have a long term future with the organisation. Short term fluctuations can be met with part-time or temporary staff.

Organisational expectations

What does your organisation require of you? Several basics are common to most organisations:

- only recruit someone if it is necessary
- only recruit someone if they have the necessary skills and abilities
- treat applicants with courtesy and respect – besides being the decent thing to do, your applicants might also be your customers
- treat all applicants fairly
- be efficient in the management of the process
- remember that you are a representative of the organisation.

In addition to these 'basics', you need to align your actions with any organisational initiatives that might be happening or about to happen.

Organisational initiatives

41

Four of the more likely organisational initiatives that you might have to incorporate into your organisational entry process at present are:

- diversity analysis
- competency planning
- training and development opportunities
- corporate advertising.

Diversity analysis   Many organisations are now looking at the balance of their workforce to see whether it reflects the balance of the wider community. This is being done for a number of reasons. Perhaps the most prominent reason is that a workforce which reflects the community is viewed as more creative, innovative, and more likely to produce and deliver products and services required by the community.

In chapter 2, I looked at fair organisational entry and said that it is unlawful to discriminate positively in favour of any racial group. However, I also said that it is lawful to take positive action so that applicants are encouraged from the under-represented groups that you wish to recruit. Such diversity initiatives are not always publicised. But you need to know if any exist so that you might take appropriate action.

An additional enquiry you should make concerns any responsibilities you might have towards people with disabilities. As mentioned in chapter 2, there has been a legal obligation for organisations to ensure that at least 3% of their workforce comprised people with disabilities. What other factors must you now take into account under the new Disability Act?

Competency planning Organisations have taken different approaches to competency. Some simply view competencies as a development of skill and ability identification. Others use them as a way of assessing staff development needs. And yet others view competencies as a framework for human resource management. In this case, employees are seen as assets rather than costs. Employers have to invest in them so they can add value to the organisation. People, after all, make the decisions in organisations. What they decide is central to the organisation's performance.

If your organisation is interested in competencies, whatever its approach, it will have implications for your organisational entry. It might be that you have to add some competencies to your selection criteria, such as proficiency in a second language as a desirable skill, it might be that there are future change programmes that will affect the newcomer's job, or it might be that the organisation is keen to recruit certain skills which might dovetail with your vacancy.

Training and development opportunities One of the questions that interviewees frequently ask concerns how the job will develop: 'what opportunities are there for development?' Interviewers are also interested in this: 'where do you see yourself in five years time?' You need to know what opportunities there are for training and development. This will also help you determine which of your selection criteria are more important; some weaknesses in applicants can be overcome by in-house training.

Of equal importance is the fact that the absence of training and development opportunities is an important reason for people leaving organisations. Lack of training also leads to employees fitting the organisation less well.

Corporate advertising Many organisations choose to advertise themselves when they advertise a job. This has mixed blessings, as I will show in chapter 6, but if it is something your organisation does then you will need to incorporate it into your advertising.

What organisational issues must you take into account?

Make a note in your diary to fix a meeting with the personnel department to discuss how your planned organisational entry activity fits in with other plans and initiatives.

Workforce planning

Usually workforce planning is carried out at an organisational level. However, if you are recruiting staff for your team, you need to understand its staffing requirements for the foreseeable future. In this way you ensure that you don't recruit when there isn't a need, and also that you don't try to make do with existing resources when the sensible thing would be to get another member of staff. There are ways to forecast your team's staffing needs.

Most managers do very little to assess whether or not they need to recruit another member of staff. Instead, the need to recruit someone usually emerges gradually, or is the automatic response to someone leaving. Consequently, it is all too easy to make hasty decisions that ignore internal candidates and the possibilities for redesigning the job. Before you decide to find a new member of staff for your team, first ask yourself the following question: 'would I want to join this team/organisation given the amount of manpower planning that has taken place?' Remember that starting a new job is a highly stressful experience, and one that greatly affects people's lives.

What are your team's staffing requirements?

Three questions combine to reveal a lot of information about the staffing requirements of your team.

- What are the objectives of the team?
- What tasks must the team complete?
- What skills (or competencies) are needed within the team to complete these tasks?

The answers to these questions produce a lot of information about the current functions and purpose of your team. To turn this into a 'team workforce plan' you must ask a further series of questions:

Does your team need another person?

- How are the objectives of the team likely to change in the foreseeable future?
- What tasks are already performed well by team members?
- Which of the skills (or competencies) are held by team members?
- What are the training needs of existing team members?
- What are the pressures for and against changing the jobs of existing team members?
- What changes in the internal environment can you foresee?
- What changes in the external environment can you foresee?
- How might technological changes affect working patterns?
- How might you lose staff to other teams or organisations?

In short, to create your team's manpower plan, you need to analyse whether the existing skill requirements, tasks and objectives are being satisfied. Then you need to carry out an analysis of change to see how these existing requirements might alter over the foreseeable future. Let me illustrate how this could work with an example.

Imagine a typical finance department in a medium sized financial services company. The department has eleven members of staff and is headed by Paul, the finance director. Under him, David, a qualified financial accountant looks after the financial accounts. A qualified management accountant, Sheena, is responsible for the management accounts and management information.

David, the financial accountant, has two assistants who look after the bank reconciliation and the purchase ledger. Nick, a temporary member of staff, is a qualified financial accountant hired for six months from a local agency. He has been helping to reconcile the bank accounts.

Sheena, the management accountant, has a part-qualified senior analyst (Peter) and three other analysts reporting to her. The department also has a secretary (Sylvia) who reports directly to David.

David tells Paul that he is leaving to become financial controller at another financial services company. Paul must find a replacement. He has the following options:

- recruit Nick (the temporary financial accountant) to a full time post – he is well liked, has the necessary skills to do the job and has been the financial accountant's 'right hand man'
- recruit externally for a replacement
- restructure the department making Sheena (the management accountant) a financial controller with day-to-day responsibility for both financial and management accounts – this would require the recruitment of a less senior financial accountant and the promotion of Peter (the senior analyst) to management accountant if he qualifies in two months time
- give the job of financial accountant to Sheena, who is keen to broaden her role, and recruit a replacement for her, or promote Peter, when qualified, and recruit a replacement from either the analysts inside the company or from external sources
- fill the post of financial accountant with a contract or temporary member of staff – this has the benefit of speed, flexibility and lowering fixed costs
- do nothing.

Each of these options has its advantages and drawbacks. Perhaps the first two would be the natural course of action for many people with this type of problem. The biggest drawback is likely to be the adverse impact on the motivation of other team members. Whereas options that involve restructuring might lead to other unforeseen problems related to the management of change. What is Paul to do? He can find a solution by carrying out an analysis of the team.

● What are the objectives of the team?

The finance team has several urgent challenges in the following areas: reconciliation of the bank accounts which have been in a mess from 'day one', and have already attracted the attention of the auditors – a qualified audit would be a disaster; the analysis of bad debt; the development of detailed financial analysis. The chief executive has made it very clear to Paul that the generation of accurate and timely management information is imperative. The longer term objectives of the team will be the production of 'unqualified' financial accounts, regular management accounts and financial analysis as required. Paul believes that the analytical aspect will increasingly dominate the team's work as the financial and management accounting output becomes more and more automated.

● What tasks must the team complete?

The team has three main tasks: preparation of financial and management accounts and *ad hoc* management analysis. Of these, senior management is pressing for greater emphasis to be placed on the analysis of current working practices, results, and alternative courses of action to improve further the firm's competitive advantage.

● What skills are needed within the team to complete the tasks?

To handle the problems on the financial accounting side, the skills typically associated with a qualified ACA auditor are needed for two reasons: strong reconciliation skills and to give confidence to the auditors that the bank account problem is being urgently addressed. To continue the development of the management accounts, the job holder needs a thorough understanding of the working of the organisation, well developed management and financial accounting skills, ideally with an ACCA or ICMA qualification, and to be fully conversant with computerised accounts. The financial analysis section needs someone who understands the macro and micro issues that affect the profitability of an organisation. These skills would normally be found in an MBA who has worked in the area of financial analysis. It would be very advanta-

45

geous if someone in this team understood the Consumer Credit Act and other related legislation and was strong in statistical analysis.

Which of these skills does Paul have in his team? The current management accountant, Sheena, qualified as an ACA with one of the 'big' firms in the City. The temporary accountant, Nick, is also a qualified ACA. The senior analyst, Peter, should pass his ACCA examinations in a couple of months. One of the analysts in the team is half way through her studies for an MBA from the Open University. These people also bring a broad range of well developed computer skills – micro, mini and mainframe – to the team.

This analysis seems to compel a solution: promote Sheena, whom Paul would like to promote in any case, to the new post of financial controller with responsibility for both financial and management accounts. Her strong accounting skills are needed to help resolve the bank reconciliation problem and to follow through the computerisation and development of the management accounts.

Nick, the temporary accountant, can be retained as a temporary member of staff, but given the job of financial accountant and tasked with sorting out the bank accounts. This gives Paul flexibility in case the computerisation of the accounts and resolution of the bank account problem means that in six months or so the team would be over-resourced or, possibly, under-resourced. Peter, the senior analyst, can be promoted to management accountant in recognition of passing his examinations. By chance, Paul has been given the opportunity to plan and develop the careers of his staff.

However, the analysis has revealed a large hole in the team's skills: skills related to financial analysis. At present, the team is not supplying the information that senior management require. Given that this has become a priority for the organisation, Paul needs to assess in detail the long term staffing requirements for this section of his team. But he's probably best advised to treat this matter as a separate issue.

Paul analysed the problem by asking questions related to the tasks, skills and objectives of the team. He then generated a list of options. The best was chosen, i.e. creating a new position of financial controller and giving it to the current management accountant, and slightly amending the option to fit the criteria. In this example, by following a rational and systematic decision-making procedure Paul found that what had initially seemed a straightforward problem – the replacement of the financial accountant – was not the real problem. He had the skills in the team to accomplish all the financial accounting tasks effectively. Instead, he found that the real problem concerned the lack of analytical skills.

The cost benefit analysis of effective organisational entry

■ ■ ■

I am frequently asked if it is worth spending all the time, money and effort that this systematic approach to organisational entry entails. At the start of the book, I looked at the cost of recruiting someone on a three year contract at £17,000. I estimated that the cost of the person to the organisation would be in the region of £100,000 without adding in the costs or profits from the person's actions.

Obviously, the amount that you spend varies on the circumstances. But most experts now believe that money spent in this field is one of the best investments an organisation can make.

How big is your investment decision?

What is the newcomer's probable starting salary?	(1)	£ _____
How much annual bonus will they get?	(2)	£ _____
How long will they stay with the organisation?	(3)	_____years
What's the average wage of managers in your organisation?	(4)	£ _____
How many hours of managerial time will be used?	(5)	_____ hours
How much will be spent on consultants?	(6)	£ _____
How much will be spent on advertising?	(7)	£ _____
How much will be spent on the administration of entry?	(8)	£ _____
How much will be spent on training each year?	(9)	£ _____
Salary of newcomer (1) x (3) years of service =	(a)	£ _____
Bonus (2) x (3) years of service =	(b)	£ _____
Employers N.I. contributions (approx.) = (a+b) x 0.12 =	(c)	£ _____
Training costs (9) x (3) =	(d)	£ _____
Extra staff related costs (a) x 2 =	(e)	£ _____
Total staff related costs (a+b+c+d+e) =	(f)	£ _____
Money spent on consultants (6) =	(g)	£ _____
Money spent on advertising (7) =	(h)	£ _____
Average salary ((4)/1680) x (5) hours spent on entry	(i)	£ _____
Administrative costs (8) =	(j)	£ _____
Total organisational entry costs (g+h+i+j) =	(k)	£ _____
Total investment (f) + (k) =	(l)	£ _____

Remember that training costs should involve the cost of trainers etc. and that the administrative costs should include the time of the staff involved as well as stationery and postage. Also, when calculating the managerial time involved in organisational entry, be sure to include all the time spent on the process, including shortlisting, briefing consultants, conducting job analyses and so on. The extra staff related costs include computers, floor space, furniture and so on. This calculation considerably underesti-mates the size of the investment decision as it ignores the likelihood of the person being promoted or receiving salary increases above the rate of inflation. It also excludes benefits from recruiting high performers.

What is the cost benefit of recruiting excellent people?

In the previous activity you calculated the size of the investment that you are about to make, regardless of considerations of how well the new recruit performs. Research into the benefits of recruiting effective staff has shown that the difference between recruiting highly effective rather than less effective supervisors can be 40% of salary per annum. You can use this research finding to improve your estimation of the size of your investment.

Direct staff costs = (a)+(b)+(c)	(m)	£ _____
40% of the direct staff costs = (m) x 0.4	(n)	£ _____
Total investment	(l)	£ _____
Investment cost of a less effective recruit = (l) + ((n) / 2)	(o)	£ _____
Investment cost of a highly effective recruit = (l) – ((n) / 2)	(p)	£ _____
Cost benefit of effective recruitment = (o) – (p)		£ _____

Please bear in mind that these figures are only intended to give you a feel for the size of your investment and the rough cost benefit of using appropriate recruitment and selection techniques. This is just one way to calculate these figures. If you would like to examine the financial side of organisational entry in greater depth you need to study a subject called utility analysis. Most good books in the field cover this area. A good one to start with would be Smith and Robertson (1993). You can find the full reference at the back of this book.

48

SUMMARY – CHAPTER 4 *APPROACH*

- Short term recruitment strategies lead to:
  - recruitment costs
  - training costs
  - redundancy and outplacement costs
  - disruption costs
  - learning curve costs
  - wasted managerial time
  - a less committed workforce.

- Your organisation expects you to:
  - recruit only when necessary
  - recruit the best person with suitable skills and abilities
  - treat applicants with courtesy and respect
  - treat all applicants fairly
  - be efficient in the management of the process.

- You should analyse the objectives, tasks and skills of your team before recruiting a new employee.

- Organisational entry decisions are big decisions.

49

5
■ ■ ■

How to analyse jobs, organisations, and change

CHAPTER OBJECTIVES

When you have read this chapter, you should be able to:

- analyse a job that you wish to fill to reveal the required knowledge, skills, abilities and other characteristics
- design a new job so that the incumbent performs well and gains satisfaction from their work
- detail those aspects of your organisation's culture that newcomers must be able to cope with to perform effectively
- describe a job that you wish to fill and produce selection criteria for a vacant job
- analyse how the jobs of existing staff will change.

CHAPTER OVERVIEW

In this chapter, I focus on what is probably the most important stage of organisational entry: the analysis stage. If you get this wrong your mistakes cascade down through the whole organisational entry process. You need to analyse three things: the job, the organisation, and how your planned change will affect others. In this chapter, I demonstrate that you already have the skills and abilities required to do this. But to help you further, I look at a structured way of analysing organisational entry needs which includes observation, structured interviews, checklists, and the analysis of critical incidents.

The importance of analysis
■ ■ ■

A nalysis is probably the most important stage of organisational entry. Unfortunately, it is also the stage that is most commonly overlooked.

> 'Maureen, we have to find a replacement for Janice. Could you phone up the agencies and get some CVs?'
>
> 'Yes Alison, what do you need the person to do?'
>
> 'The same things that Janice did. You know, word processing, answering the phone, taking messages, the normal things that secretaries do.'
>
> 'Can you be a bit more specific, that's a bit vague?'
>
> 'Come on, we all know what secretaries do. Just get some people in for me to see. You'll give 'em a typing test, won't you?'

51

This sort of exchange is typical of much organisational entry analysis. It is not surprising really, given that the culture of many organisations puts managers in 'power' roles where they are expected to know all about their subordinates. Managers cannot admit to not knowing what their staff do.

This problem masks the complexity in people's jobs. No one could expect to understand fully every subordinate's job on a constant basis, especially as jobs are continually changing and evolving for all manner of reasons. In the previous example, for instance, Janice didn't just do the typing. She also managed the itineraries of the ten people in the department, organised travel plans, originated new designs for presentations, downloaded information from the mainframe, and carried out some numerical analysis. More than this though, Janice was the hub of the department around which everything revolved. She organised office 'get togethers', kept everyone's spirits up when the managing director announced his latest crazy initiative, and had excellent contacts with other departments. Janice also did some typing, answered the phone, and took messages.

By not understanding fully the complexity of Janice's job, Alison was unlikely to find a suitable replacement. She might have found someone good at typing and with a strong telephone personality, but it would have been chance if she had recruited someone capable of performing the ancillary tasks to the same level, although differently, as Janice.

> **If you don't know what you're looking for how can you expect to find it?**

An overview of organisational entry analysis

Analysis is all about understanding. The purpose of carrying it out is to discover how the job holder interacts with their job and the environment in which the job is set. Following a rational approach, this analysis is translated into a set of selection criteria which are used to:

- determine what recruitment methods are likely to attract suitably qualified applicants
- determine which selection techniques are likely to be appropriate
- decide which applicant has the best fit to the job and the organisation's culture.

Job descriptions are an important intermediate stage in the development of selection criteria as they allow you to check that the job you're looking to fill is complete. They can also be given to applicants, to help them to decide whether they wish to continue with their application.

However, job descriptions do have some drawbacks. They can encourage you to think of the job in terms of its duties and responsibilities and to forget about other important issues when creating your selection criteria. To guard against this, it is useful to return to your original data and use them with the job description when producing selection criteria.

You have probably heard of personnel specifications (or job or person specifications) in connection with organisational entry. Most writers on recruitment or selection describe how to produce a personnel specification as an integral part of the process between job descriptions and the selection criteria (or, as a surrogate for the selection criteria). This is *not* the approach I take.

I see personnel specifications as useful in their own context. Personnel specifications are communications to a personnel department concerning your requirements. Unfortunately, when considering whom to recruit, they can get in the way if you're doing the work yourself. The goal of organisational entry analysis is to understand fully the nature of the job and convert this understanding into a set of criteria that can be used later in the process. By first converting the analysis into a personnel specification, you complicate the process and this can have four detrimental effects:

- important factors are given incorrect emphasis as they move from piece of paper to piece of paper

- personnel specifications encourage the analyst to record tasks, skills and responsibilities rather than developing a broader understanding of the role
- the task of producing three separate reports can be off putting and discourage the manager from carrying out any analysis at all
- most importantly, personnel specifications tend to simplify the process and eliminate the crucial understanding of complexity in jobs.

The analysis phase of organisational entry can be illustrated as shown in Figure 5.1.

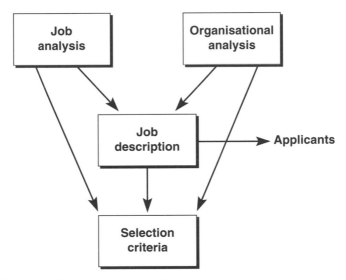

53

Fig 5.1 The organisational entry analysis process

What job do you wish to analyse?

The rest of this book contains a series of exercises that ask you to analyse a job, choose suitable recruitment and selection techniques, and plan introduction and socialisation events. You can use these to help internalise the ideas, or to help you find a new member of staff. Decide now which job(s) you wish to analyse.

Job analysis

■ ■ ■

Why doesn't job analysis get carried out by managers? Earlier, I suggested that it might have something to do with managers being afraid to admit that they don't fully appreciate the nature of their subordinates' jobs. Perhaps managers assume they know what their staff do. Another reason might be that job analysis is seen as a time-consuming and laborious task with minimal benefit. Alternatively, some managers view job analysis as a complex specialist skill which they are unable to perform. I hope that I have already dispelled the first two assumptions. I now hope to dismiss the third and fourth reasons as well.

Analysing your own job

Imagine that you are looking to recruit someone to fill your job. How would you analyse your job? What could you do?

> It might seem a little strange analysing your own job. But the point of this exercise is to pause for a moment to think how you can gather information about a job and to illustrate that you already have most of the skills required to analyse a job thoroughly. For example, you might have mentioned that you could observe yourself at work, you could interview yourself, you could ask yourself to supply a report about the job, you could ask others about the work you do, or you could look at some of the work that you have produced. These are the main methods of job analysis.

There are no great secrets to job analysis; anyone can do it. However, that said, haphazard investigation leads to a haphazard job description and selection criteria. It is useful, therefore, to have a structure around which to base your analysis. Karl Popper, a leading philosopher, used to demonstrate this point during lectures. He would say to the audience, 'Observe!' To which the instant and automatic reply was 'Observe what?' A framework will give you guidance concerning what you should look for when conducting a job analysis.

A framework for job analysis

Broadly speaking, there are three ways that you can approach job analysis. Fortunately, these are not mutually exclusive and each will yield different insights and information regarding the job. You need to use these three approaches together because a dependence on any one will skew the analysis.

> When analysing a job you need to understand:
>
> 1 the *tasks* the job holder will have to do
> 2 the *skills* the job holder will need
> 3 the *roles* the job holder has to fill.

There are ways you can embellish the framework. For example, if the job requires the person to make decisions you might also want to think about:

- the alternatives they have to choose between
- the demands placed on the decision maker
- the constraints they will be under.

Or you might want to break down each of the components of the job analysis framework into smaller constituent parts. You might also want to investigate the knowledge a newcomer would need to bring to the job, the experience they must have, and so on.

55

But a word of warning: make sure that your job analysis is relevant to performance – you want to avoid superfluous factors that will affect your ability to find the best person. Constantly ask yourself (or the job holder if there is one): how important is this factor for performance? This helps separate out the essential from the less critical factors.

> **Job analysis is all about revealing the factors in a job relevant to performance.**

The job analysis framework in operation

This all sounds fine, but what does it mean in practice? Is it important to analyse a job from these three different perspectives?

Steve is a shift manager in a retail distribution warehouse. The warehouse receives bulk supplies of products from a number of companies around Europe. These bulk deliveries are then divided into individual order quantities for retail outlets of a large shopping chain with 400 stores around the UK. The individual orders are then dispatched to each store. The company works twenty-four hours a day with three eight-hour shifts. Steve is the shift manager for the day shift on the clothing side. He has applied for, and been given, a promotion. He has been asked to find a replacement for himself. Rather than jump to conclusions, he decides to use the framework for job analysis to help him understand his job better.

The tasks

On a day-to-day basis, Steve has to manage twenty staff on every shift. He has three supervisors to help him. His first task every day is to discuss any problems that may have arisen on the previous shift with that shift's manager. Steve then plans his staffing roster for the day. This is followed by a meeting with his supervisors where they discuss the work schedules and staffing. During the day Steve's role is to ensure the smooth running of the shift, and most of the tasks he gets involved in are concerned with minor problems as they arise. Towards the end of the day, Steve prepares a report for the manager on the next shift.

Steve also has to produce regular reports on the department and control a budget. He attends briefing meetings and passes on the main points to the rest of his shift. He also gets involved in organisational entry for the company and with the introduction and training of newcomers to his team.

The skills

Steve found it more difficult to identify the skills he uses. But of the ones he could identify, he thought the following were the more important:

- the ability to motivate the people in his team
- knowledge of the operation and the process
- the ability to train people
- diplomacy (as he is involved in answering queries from the customer)
- communication skills
- common sense
- chairing meetings
- problem solving
- report writing
- interpretation of numerical information.

When he reviewed the list, he felt that the first five items were the most important to have.

The roles

Steve was even less clear about the roles that he was required to fill. So he dropped in on the personnel director. To his surprise, he found that he is responsible for health and safety issues during his shifts. He also has responsibilities in case of fire. He has to fill in certain forms relating to attendance, holidays and the like. He is also responsible for any over or underspends on the department budget. But his main role is that of the person responsible for the shift – the person whom people on the warehouse floor can come to for help and advice.

So what does this example show? The purpose of relating it is to demonstrate that if you look at a job from different perspectives, you will come to different conclusions about the nature of the job. Had Steve just focused on the tasks he carries out, he would have missed the diversity of skills that he uses and some of the special roles that the organisation gives him. The lesson from this example is that you need to analyse your job from all three perspectives.

Methods of data collection

The previous example focused on the job holder's own job. Unfortunately, when you look at the jobs of others, you can't use your own direct experience to inform your analysis. Instead you have to carry out an investigation. There are a number of different ways of collecting data about a job, each with its strengths and weaknesses.

Observation

If you are trying to fill a job which someone is already doing, watching the person at work is a natural way to gain an understanding of the position. However, as Popper suggested, you need a framework around which to base your observations. This is simply achieved by writing the words 'Tasks', 'Skills', 'Roles', and 'Other' on your notepad. And when you see things relevant to one of the categories, you note it down. Simple as that.

The drawbacks of observation

Can you identify three possible disadvantages of observation as a means of job analysis?

Observation, the simplest and most straightforward job analysis tool, has some major limitations.

- *The time it can take. Unless the job has very little variety of tasks, skills or roles, observation of all the features of the job can take a considerable amount of time. For example, some tasks might be carried out once a month. No one has the time (or patience) to sit and observe someone for this long.*

- *The observer may not be aware of many of the things that the job holder might be doing. You could observe someone word processing documents, but might miss the fact that they were rearranging the presentation, improving the grammar, checking the spelling and so on.*
- *Being observed can be quite uncomfortable and might lead to the job holder changing the way they do things. They might be on their best behaviour which could give you a misleading impression of the job.*
- *Observation is unlikely to produce an understanding of the comparative importance of the actions and behaviours seen.*
- *The current job holder may not be very good at the job. This could cause the observer to lower their expectations and lead to the continuation of poor performance in the job.*
- *It doesn't take into account how the job might be about to change.*

However, observation is a good way to get an overview of a job, and it is very useful when the job is fairly static and doesn't have much variety or complication.

Self-descriptions, diaries and logs

Self-descriptions, diaries, and logs are a variation on observation. Rather than sitting watching the person doing the job, which can be time consuming, dull, and offer only a partial impression, you could ask the person to record what it is they do.

Self-descriptions have several advantages:

- they are the least disruptive method as you can ask the person to write their description at a convenient moment
- they record the incumbent's own perceptions of the job
- if there are many people doing the job and describing it, you are likely to get quite a good overview.

However there are several drawbacks:

- the person might not be completely honest in their description
- they might focus on the tasks or skills and not cover other important topics
- there is a tendency for people to focus on those points that they think are important, rather than describing a fuller picture

■ the information generated is likely to be somewhat unstructured, which will probably give you problems interpreting it

■ the person simply might not be very good at communicating the nature of their job.

Diaries and logs are very similar, except that they have a slightly more structured approach. They take longer, but usually supply better quality data. They generally have the same pluses and minuses as self-descriptions.

In what circumstances are these techniques useful? As you might imagine, they are designed to be used for understanding quite complex jobs which it is impractical to analyse through observation. The descriptions, diaries and logs allow the job holder to record events over an extended period. But the biggest drawback is that the descriptions are unlikely to be complete. These techniques are quite useful, then, as a precursor to more detailed analysis through interviews.

Interviews

In practice, when you observe someone at work you usually also ask them some questions to clarify what you have seen and resolve any misunderstandings. More importantly, job analysis interviews allow you to probe into the comparative importance of parts of the job and to see the job as the job holder sees it. Of course, this might not be the whole picture, but it's a good place to start.

Job analysis interviews have several major advantages:

■ they are suitable for a large number of jobs providing there is someone around who has done the job before

■ they are relatively quick and easy

■ they allow you to probe into all sorts of issues

■ structured interview plans are available that can help you cover most of the salient points.

You can use the following series of topics and questions to structure your job analysis interview.

A STRUCTURED JOB ANALYSIS INTERVIEW

Setting the scene
1 What is your job title?
2 Where do you work?
3 To whom do you report?
4 Who works for you?
5 What are your main objectives and goals?
6 To whom do you spend most of your time communicating?

Tasks and associated skills
1 How would you describe your job?
2 What do you spend most of your time doing?
3 How would you divide up your time amongst these tasks?
4 Which of the tasks are most important?
5 Which of the tasks must be done?
6 Do you choose to do any tasks that you don't have to?
7 Why do you choose to do this extra work?
8 What written work do you have to do?
9 What level of literacy is required? Why?
10 What physical work do you have to do?
11 What creative work do you have to do?
12 What numerical work do you have to do?
13 What level of numeracy is needed? Why?
14 What mechanical work do you have to do?
15 What presentations do you have to give? How often? Why?
16 What presentation or communication skills are required?
17 Do you buy anything? What? How often?
18 Do you sell anything? What? How often?
19 What buying or selling skills do you need?
20 Do you get involved in organisational entry? How often? For what positions?
21 What organisational entry skills do you need?
22 What are the consequences of not completing these tasks? For you? For others? For the organisation?

Other skills
1 What level of education do you need? Why?
2 What computer skills are needed? Why?
3 What skills of organisation are required to do this job? Why?
4 If machinery is used, what mechanical skills are required?
5 Do you have to solve problems? What sort? What skills are required to solve them?
6 Do you need high levels of physical fitness or strength to do this job? Why? Quantify.
7 What other skills do you need to do this job? Why?
8 What experience do you need to do this job? Why?

60

9   How long would it take to gain this experience?
10 Where could this experience be gained? Where else?
11 Do you have to train anyone? In what skills?
12 In what ways could this job be done differently?
13 Which of the skills you've mentioned are essential?
14 Which of the essential skills could be acquired quickly on the job?
15 Which of the essential skills could be acquired quickly with training?
16 What would make it difficult to perform well in this job? Why?

Roles
1   What formal roles do you fill?
2   Whom do you supervise? How much time and effort does this consume?
3   What is the role of your boss? How much contact is there between you? How accessible and supportive is your boss?
4   How does your boss determine your performance?
5   How else might your boss determine your performance?
6   How do you prioritise your work?
7   What planning do you have to do?
8   What money or assets are you responsible for? What does this involve?
9   Are you responsible for anyone's safety? What does this involve?
10 Do you have to have any professional qualifications for this job? Which ones? Why?
11 Do you have to have any other qualifications for this job?

Other
1   What decisions do you have to make?
2   What choices can you make?
3   What constraints do you have upon you?
4   What demands are made of you?
5   What forms of communication do you use?
6   How is your job different now to when you began doing it? For what reasons has it changed?
7   How have you changed your job?
8   How could you develop the job?
9   How is the job likely to change?
10 Is there anything else that I haven't covered?

You will see that many of the questions are overlapping and the decision regarding which category to put some of them into is a little arbitrary. You will need to edit out some of the questions as they will clearly be superfluous. Nevertheless, these questions provide a useful framework around which to shape a job analysis interview. Another benefit is that they can also be used by the analyst to investigate the shape of new jobs. But more on this later.

Asking someone all these questions will clearly be quite time-consuming. More than this though, an enormous amount of data is likely to be generated. This causes two problems. First the problem of gathering it all. It can be very handy tape recording and transcribing job analysis interviews; this frees you to concentrate on what the person is saying and ensures that you capture all the key points. It is also useful evidence in case you are accused of unfair discrimination. The second problem is that the sheer volume of data can mask or lose key bits of information. Consequently, it is advisable to ask the interviewee to pick out the most important bits and to rank or order things wherever possible.

Whom to interview?

So far I have assumed that you would want to interview the person currently doing the job. But when you thought about your own job, you probably indicated that there are a number of other people who could give you valuable information about the key characteristics. Perhaps you included your boss, your customers, your suppliers, or your staff. All these people are likely to give you very different perspectives which increase your understanding of the job.

Who knows the England football manager's job?

Imagine that you have been asked to find the next England football manager. Whom would you interview as part of your job analysis? Try to identify five different people or positions that you would like to talk to. Try to think how each person's perspective might differ.

The purpose of this exercise is to illustrate the point that the people who interact with the job holder are likely to hold different perspectives regarding the real nature of the job. For instance, you might have mentioned the players. They want a manager who is fair and who motivates. The Football Association, on the other hand, is probably much more concerned with results. Managers of football league clubs are more interested in the ability of the manager to prepare the squad with minimal interference to the domestic league programme. Whilst TV pundits might continually reflect on the artistry of the front players and the solidity of the 'back four'. If you spoke to previous incumbents of the job, you might find that they stress the need to manage the media above footballing considerations. The press, meanwhile, might talk in noble terms about the importance of the manager bringing back self-respect to the nation (whilst preparing their 'Atkinson is an Artichoke' headlines). And, if this were being conducted for real, no one would ask the fans (customers).

Whom do you need to interview?

For the job that you are analysing, who might have interesting insights about it that you would want to talk to?

Critical incidents

The critical incident interviewing technique can be useful for job analysis and selection interviewing. In essence, it is an interviewing technique that focuses on events that have been important in determining whether the job holder was successful, or not, in accomplishing their goals.

The interviewer starts by asking 'could you give me an example of an incident when something went particularly well, and this helped you meet your objectives, or when you did something extremely badly, and you did not meet your objectives?' After the interviewee has given an example, the interviewer follows up by probing deeper into the causes, consequences, and implications of the incidents. The interviewer repeats this for as long as the interviewee can think of incidents to relate.

> 1 Could you give me an example of an incident when something went particularly well and this helped you meet your objectives?
> 2 Could you give me an example of an incident when something went particularly badly and this caused you to fail to meet your objectives?

The description should include several items:

- an incident that led to the person achieving, or failing to achieve, an objective
- the background and context of the incident
- what the person actually did, or failed to do, that caused them to achieve, or fail to achieve, their objective
- when the incident happened, whether it happens regularly, and whether it might happen again.

One of the strengths of the critical incident approach is that it can be used in conjunction with the other methods already described. It is likely to be useful because it will give you some guidance as to the priority and comparative importance of the various factors mentioned by the interviewee. It also has the benefit of being suitable for use in a high proportion of job analysis exercises.

But the critical incident technique isn't perfect and probably wouldn't be used in isolation. It tends to ignore the mundane things that people do which are an integral part of jobs and it is a technique that many people find difficult to use. On one occasion when I used the technique, the job holder couldn't think of any critical incidents at all. This is not unusual, especially when you are analysing administrative or solitary jobs. Furthermore, many people are unwilling to recount the incidents that really show them in a bad light. Consequently, it can sometimes give you a glamorised impression of the job. That said, the critical incident technique is quick and easy to use and can be tagged on to the end of a normal job analysis interview. It's always worth giving it a go: you might be surprised at its power.

64

Steve, the shift manager at the retail distribution warehouse, also analysed his own job using the critical incident technique. He thought to himself, *'what incidents can I think of when something went particularly well, and this helped me meet my objectives?'*. He remembered the occasion when his main contact at the customer called to remonstrate about a delivery failure of a product being launched that day. Steve calmed the customer down and then made strenuous efforts to arrange a special delivery via taxi. The product arrived in time to be on the shelves before the store opened. Ever since then, Steve has had the impression that he is the person the customer most trusts and wants to talk to if there is a problem. This trust, which has matured into mutual respect, has been useful to Steve on many occasions (he noted down exactly where and when) because it has enabled him to 'work around' any distribution difficulties, such as the breakdown of lorries, whilst not incurring the wrath of the customer. This is particularly important in Steve's situation because one of his key objectives is to satisfy the customer's needs. From this incident, Steve inferred that the ability to form effective working relationships with third parties was a key part of his job. He was able to think of four more examples of positive critical incidents.

He then thought to himself, *'what incidents can I think of when something went extremely badly that caused me to fail to meet my objectives?'*. Rather embarrassingly, the incident of the court case immediately sprang to mind. One of Steve's duties is to record the arrival of goods inwards. Occasionally he has to arrange transportation for these goods. On one occasion, there was confusion over the method of charging. Was it ex-works or FOB? The courier company insisted that ex-works terms had been agreed that meant that Steve's company had to pick up the freight charges. It couldn't be agreed amicably and the courier company took legal action in the small claims court to get its £112.30. It won, principally because Steve was unable to provide documentary evidence to support his view of events. Although the incident had been embarrassing for Steve, it had only a small impact on his appraisal. But it taught him the importance of accurate record keeping and administration in all matters, and he now believed this to be a key component of the job. Steve was able to think of two more negative examples.

This example illustrates that the critical incident technique can yield a different pattern of insights about a job to observation or interviews. However, they are not mutually exclusive. Indeed, the combination of all three methods usually makes for a most effective job analysis exercise. Observation tends to inform the interview. And the interview produces a lot of information which the critical incident technique often helps to prioritise and evaluate.

Other methods

There are many other job analysis techniques around. However, most require training or have to be bought commercially. Examples are adjective checklists (where you show a list of words to a job holder and ask them how each word might inform you about their job), questionnaires (these have now been produced for all manner of jobs), and checklists and inventories. If you find that the methods described in this chapter are not sufficient or appropriate for your needs, then you might want to investigate some of these further. A good place to start looking for these methods is a trade journal such as *People Management*. But, unfortunately, a discussion of each of these methods is beyond the scope of this book.

When the job is a new one

All the job analysis techniques discussed so far assume that there is someone currently doing the job, or with intimate knowledge of it, whom you can observe and talk to. However, a large number of vacancies are new jobs which haven't previously existed. How do you go about analysing these? There are two principal ways to do this:

- job analysis
- models of job design.

Job analysis for new jobs

How can the job analysis techniques we've already looked at help you understand jobs that have never existed before? The structured interview and the critical incident technique can actually be quite useful. Assuming that you have a basic idea about the nature of the job (e.g. 'we need someone else on the purchase ledger', 'Helen needs a secretary') these techniques will help inform you of its detail.

You begin by getting together people most likely to have knowledge of the job. If Helen needs a secretary, then Helen, a secretary doing a similar job, and maybe someone from the personnel department should meet. You then run through the structured interview plan and try to predict how the incumbent would answer the questions. Then try to predict what sort of incidents would be critical to the success or failure of the employee. In this way, you gain insight into the nature of the job.

A model of job design

There are several models for the design of jobs. You might have heard of Frederick Taylor who concentrated on shop floor workers on production lines, or Frederick Herzberg, who looked at how characteristics of jobs influenced the satisfaction and dissatisfaction levels of workers. If you are interested in job design and worker motivation, then you might like to follow up on these two researchers. However I shall concentrate on Richard Hackman and Greg Oldham as their work separates out five core job dimensions that, they say, all jobs should possess if they are to motivate and satisfy the worker and lead to a higher quality of performance and lower turnover of staff.

These core job dimensions are:

- **skill variety** – how many different skills and abilities does the job require?
- **task identity** – to what extent is the job 'whole and meaningful'?
- **task significance** – does the job have wider significance, either to people inside the organisation or to society in general?
- **autonomy** – how much individual freedom, independence and discretion does the job holder have in carrying out their work?
- **feedback** – how much information does the job holder get about their level of performance?

Hackman and Oldham suggest that these dimensions lead to, or induce, three critical psychological states:

- **experienced meaningfulness of the work** – to what extent does the individual find the work meaningful, valuable and worthwhile?
- **experienced responsibility for the outcomes of the work** – to what extent does the incumbent feel responsible for the work outcomes?

■ **knowledge of the actual results of the work activities – to** what extent does the job holder know and understand how well they are performing?

People who score higher on these core psychological states will probably experience more of the following than people who score lower:

■ high internal work motivation

■ high quality work performance

■ high satisfaction with the work

■ low absenteeism and staff turnover.

All five core job dimensions are important. If one is missing then it is thought that the critical psychological states will be weakened and the positive results noticeably lessened. You've probably already spotted that this model can be quite useful in assessing the quality of existing as well as new jobs.

Is your own job well designed?

67

Briefly, run through the components of Hackman and Oldham's model of job design by relating it to your own job. Is it well designed? Are any of the factors missing? What are the consequences of this?

● What skills do you use?
● Is your job 'whole and meaningful'?
● What is its significance?
● How much discretion have you over the way you do your work?
● What feedback do you get?
● Would you say that any of the five core job dimensions are weak or non-existent in your job? Which ones?
● In what ways is your job meaningful?
● In what ways do you feel responsible for your work?
● How do you find out about your level of performance?
● Which of the following apply to your own job?
 – High internal work motivation
 – High quality work performance
 – Feeling that you 'fit in'
 – High satisfaction with the work
 – Low absenteeism
 – Enjoyment from your work
 – Feeling that you want to stay with the firm

Does the theory of Hackman and Oldham highlight any weaknesses in the design of your own job? If so, what are they?

This exercise shows how the model works by applying it to an example that you know well – your own job. It also illustrates how useful the theory is for explaining the important effects on performance, satisfaction and absenteeism. It does not predict all the possible effects, nor does it include all the factors contributing towards them, but those it does include (i.e. the five core job dimensions and the critical psychological states) have been shown to be important causes of these positive effects. If you want to recruit people who'll stick around, it's a model of job design that you'll probably want to use.

But how do you use the model to understand a new job? Well, you'd probably want to start with the interview questions described a little earlier. This would give you a pretty fair understanding of the new position. You then try to analyse the new job under each of the five core job dimensions to see whether it is a 'whole'. Where there are weaknesses, you would try to work out what critical psychological states this will cause, and what the implications for organisational entry are. Is it possible to redesign the job to alleviate the problem? You should make the problem known to applicants so that they aren't recruited under a misapprehension (the quickest way to lose someone).

Managerial judgement

As with the analysis of existing jobs, the techniques for analysing new jobs are not mutually exclusive. Indeed, they are probably best used in combination. Each one will offer a different perspective and inform the other. The key point is that you need to think about the characteristics of new jobs and not just assume that their structure will emerge and evolve in the natural course of events. That is likely to lead to the incumbent drifting away from the goals and objectives of the organisation, and cause dissatisfaction, stress, and possible exit from the organisation.

> **You must analyse and design *new* jobs as well as existing jobs.**

Organisational fit analysis
■ ■ ■

In the early chapters of this book, I suggested that the biggest contribution it makes is the explicit separation of job and organisation fit in organisational entry. The idea is that behaviour at work stems from an interaction of employees and the environment in which they find themselves. Partly this relates to their fit to the job, but it is also important how people fit the organisation's culture. Consequently, if you want to recruit people who'll be motivated, experience less stress, and stick around, you need to consider both types of fit: job fit and organisational fit.

As this is quite a new idea which is being actively researched on many fronts, there are no formally accepted methods for measuring organisational fit that have been tried out in an organisational entry setting. However, there are many offshoots of the research which seem appropriate and it is these that I have adapted for use in organisational entry. The fact that these techniques haven't been as fully tested as we would like means that you have to keep in mind the fundamental rational decision making model that we looked at in chapter 3. For the purpose of this discussion, this can be broken down to three key stages.

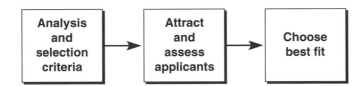

Fig 5.2 A rational selection decision

This decision making process reminds us that the reason for analysing the organisation's environment is to determine which of the applicants best fits the vacancy.

> **ORGANISATIONAL FIT ANALYSIS is the process of identifying the important factors in the environment contributing towards high levels of performance and satisfaction.**

Organisational fit and fairness

Identifying the factors outside the job that contribute to high performance and satisfaction is difficult to do fairly as it needs considerable concentration to eliminate factors that are specific to the current incumbent. You need to identify those factors that any person, regardless of gender, race, disability etc., will encounter in the job. Also you must eliminate prejudiced views: 'we need a man because it's an all male environment'. Comments such as this, which are all too common, would, if incorporated into the selection criteria, make for unlawful organisational entry.

Instead, there are gender- or race-free factors that are important for performance and satisfaction. An example might be that the department is very competitive and that this is evidenced in the reward structure which is strongly slanted towards bonuses. In such circumstances, you could safely say that any new entrant would have to relish a competitive environment and be motivated by bonuses. This would be a fair criterion and one likely to lead to the recruitment of a person able to perform and gain satisfaction in such an environment.

A framework for organisational fit analysis

Just as with job analysis, a framework is required for organisational analysis so that you know what you're looking for. The different approaches within the framework help you to look at the environment from alternative perspectives which, again, are not mutually exclusive.

Organisational culture is one of those terms that everyone seems to define differently. For me, organisational culture refers to an individual's perception of the environment in which they work. In the context of organisational entry, the perceptions of individuals are important because the outcomes we are interested in, performance, motivation, satisfaction, intentions to leave the company, commitment and so on, are all strongly influenced by people's perceptions. However, everyone is different and interacts with the environment in a different way. So, if everyone has a different view of the organisation's culture, how do you make sense of the environment to which you'll be introducing new employees?

Well, it's more straightforward than you might think. As culture is defined in terms of people's perceptions, then it follows that you need to determine the boundaries of the job holder's perceptions. With whom do they have regular contact? Who shapes the environment? If the job holder works in a team or identifiable group, does the team or group constitute the climate that the job holder works in? and so on. Each of these people has their own perspectives on their environment. You want to identify the aspects that are common to all of them, as these are likely to be key components of the job's environment.

How do you assess culture?

Imagine the job of Sarah. She is a nurse in a typical accident and emergency ward. How would you go about determining the nature of the organisational culture in which she works?

The first person to ask would be Sarah herself. How would she describe her working environment? You would ask her who she comes into contact with and you might want to observe her at work. You would then need to talk to the people Sarah mentioned. Finally, you'd compare what the various people had said and look for the common characteristics. In addition, you'd probably want to ask Sarah about a wider range of things that affect her job, such as pay systems or working conditions. It might be useful asking Sarah and her colleagues some questions about the things that give them satisfaction, pleasure, and so on. These are all likely to reveal components of the organisational culture in which Sarah's job is located.

By defining the organisational environment in terms of organisational culture, the implication is that I eliminate 'grand ideas' relating to mission or vision statements and corporate strategies, preferring to reveal those aspects of the culture that the job holder is likely to experience and be affected by personally. This, in turn, links the subjects of motivation, satisfaction, performance and, staff turnover with environmental factors. As a result, the question that you have to ask is 'what environmental factors experienced by the job holder are likely to affect their behaviour?'.

71

> **When analysing the environmental factors affecting a person at work you need to understand:**
>
> 1 interactions the job holder has with other people
> 2 reward systems and structures for compensation
> 3 values
> 4 organisation-wide initiatives
> 5 working conditions
> 6 psychological outcomes.

Clearly, there is some overlap between these environmental factors and the job factors (tasks, skills, roles) we looked at earlier. This is advantageous as it means that you can carry out job and organisational analysis simultaneously. But by separating out the two types of factors, the importance of understanding the specific skills etc. needed to do the job, and the factors that affect behaviour in the environment is highlighted.

Organisational fit analysis techniques

The purpose of organisational culture analysis is to reveal those factors outside the strict confines of the job that will significantly influence performance and satisfaction. The analysis techniques are not yet as well defined and proven as those for job analysis. Despite this, there is a variety of approaches you can use that might elicit interesting and valuable insights. The techniques fall into three categories:

- observation
- structured interviews
- checklists.

Observation

Observing the environmental factors affecting a job is just the same as observing the job itself. Observation can be more useful in this context because many of the environmental factors are easily spotted in a short period of time. The working conditions are best recorded through observation, and you can also gain some useful information on the nature of interactions with other people.

Structured interviews

Interviews are as useful for organisational analysis work as they are for job analysis. In the same way, a structured format can help you understand the environment better than if you adopt an unstructured approach.

A STRUCTURED ORGANISATIONAL ANALYSIS INTERVIEW

Interactions

1 Who inside the organisation do you come into contact with in the course of your job? For how long? How often? Where?
2 Describe the nature of these interactions. What is the subject matter?
3 How would you describe your relationship with each of the people you've mentioned?
4 Who outside the organisation do you come into contact with in the course of your job? For how long? How often? Where?
5 Describe the nature of these interactions. What is the subject matter?
6 How would you describe your relationship with each of the people you've mentioned?
7 Do you consider yourself to be part of a team or work group? If so, which teams or work groups do you belong to? What is the purpose of these teams or groups? What does being a part of these teams or groups entail?
8 Of the interactions that you've described, which occur because they have to happen as an integral part of the job, and which occur as a

consequence of friendship or proximity?

9 To improve your efficiency and effectiveness, are there any people that you should have more contact with? Who are they? How would more contact help you perform better?

10 How do your actions and behaviour affect those that you come into contact with?

11 How have you changed the environment in which you work? How has this changed your work? How has it changed the work of others?

Reward systems

1 How much are you paid? How is this made up?

2 What proportion of your financial rewards is fixed and how much is variable?

3 What would you have to do to earn more money in your job?

4 Within the organisation, what other opportunities do you have to earn money?

5 How could you lose money and benefits?

6 What are the opportunities for promotion and advancement in your job? How can this job help you in this regard?

7 How much holiday do you have? How much control do you have over when you take holidays?

8 What hours do you work? How flexible is this? How much control over your hours do you have?

9 What 'perks' of the job do you take advantage of? What other 'perks' could you take advantage of, but don't?

Values

1 What values do people share in the organisation? How do these relate to the way that work is carried out?

2 Do you experience any unusual forms of behaviour at work?

3 What behaviours do people avoid at all costs? Why?

4 Has this job helped you feel more committed to the organisation? If so, what factors contributed towards this?

Organisation-wide initiatives

1 Do you have a sense of the organisation's mission? How is this important in your work?

2 How does your job fit in with the organisation's strategy?

3 How is your job affected by changes in organisational strategy or policy?

4 Can you relate an example of how your job has altered because of a change in organisational policy or strategy?

5 What organisational initiatives are you currently aware of? How do you think these might change your job?

Working conditions

1 Describe the physical environment in which you work.

2 Are you continually interrupted in your work? Is this an inherent part of your job?

3 How could your working environment be improved to help you perform better? What implications would this have for your levels of satisfaction?

4 Do you have to attend meetings? What are these about? What is the atmosphere of the meetings you attend?

Psychological outcomes

1 What would you regard as an achievement in this job?

2 Do you get praised for performing well? Who by?

3 How do you think other people in the organisation perceive your role?

4 Which aspects of your work give you satisfaction?

5 Do you get a sense of self-respect from doing this job?

6 What have you learnt in this job? How have you developed? What were the agents or incidents that led to this development?

7 What is the most difficult aspect of your job? Why?

8 What is the most enjoyable aspect of your job? Why?

9 Which aspect of your job would you least like to lose? Why?

Other

1 Do you do anything to help the organisation outside the limits of your job description? Why do you do these things?

2 Is there anything I've missed?

74

This structured interview format will help you gain information about the environment in which the job is located. As with all structured interviews, you should feel free to deviate from it when the interviewee says something worth pursuing. Once that line of investigation is exhausted, return to the structure. The questions are there to help you, not to hinder you.

Rather than ask you to analyse a job now, which would be quite time-consuming, try the following reflective exercise which looks at the above structured interview in relation to your own job.

Understanding your fit to the environment in which you work

Look back to the structured organisational fit analysis interview. Highlight five questions that seem to show your fit to your working environment. What insights have the questions produced?

Checklists

An alternative, but not mutually exclusive, way of understanding an organisation's culture is to use checklists. Some are series of questions, rather like the structured interview questions above, some are lists of key points to work through. Others, such as the one included here, are lists of words that can be used to explore the subject.

This checklist is called the 'Organisational Culture Profile' and it was developed by three American researchers (Charles O'Reilly, Jennifer Chatman and David Caldwell) in the early 1990s. They looked at all the writings on organisational culture and found that 54 items seemed to encapsulate all its important features.

THE ORGANISATIONAL CULTURE PROFILE

1 Flexibility
2 Adaptability
3 Stability
4 Predictability
5 Being innovative
6 Being quick to take advantage of opportunities
7 A willingness to experiment
8 Risk taking
9 Being careful
10 Autonomy
11 Being rule oriented
12 Being analytical
13 Paying attention to detail
14 Being precise
15 Being team oriented
16 Sharing information freely
17 Emphasising a single culture throughout the organisation
18 Being people oriented
19 Fairness
20 Respect for the individual's rights
21 Tolerance
22 Informality
23 Being easy going
24 Being calm
25 Being supportive
26 Being aggressive
27 Decisiveness
28 Action orientation
29 Taking initiative
30 Being reflective

31 Achievement orientation
32 Being demanding
33 Taking individual responsibility
34 Having high expectations for performance
35 Opportunities for professional growth
36 High pay for good performance
37 Security of employment
38 Offers praise for good performance
39 Low level of conflict
40 Confronting conflict directly
41 Developing friends at work
41 Fitting in
43 Working in collaboration with others
44 Enthusiasm for the job
45 Working long hours
46 Not being constrained by many rules
47 An emphasis on quality
48 Being distinctive or different from others
49 Having a good reputation
50 Being socially responsible
51 Being results oriented
52 Having a clear guiding philosophy
53 Being competitive
54 Being highly organised

How do you use it? Quite simply, you run through the list and for each one ask yourself, or others in the organisation:

> ### How characteristic of the organisation's culture is this item?

You want to discover the five or six items which are most characteristic of the organisation, and the five or six which are least characteristic. You should ask several people to go through the list to ensure that your impressions of the organisation's culture are shared by others. If you're trying to fill an existing job, it would be worthwhile asking the people the current job holder interacts with to run through the list.

You can also use this list is as a framework for an organisational culture structured interview, by turning the items into questions.

Steve, our warehouse shift manager, used this technique to try to understand his own organisation's culture better. He found it quick, easy and quite powerful. First he went through the items himself. He isolated 'being careful', 'being rule oriented', 'paying attention to detail', 'security of employment', 'low level of conflict', and 'working in collaboration with others' as the most characteristic ways to describe his organisation's culture. He then isolated 'a willingness to experiment', 'risk taking', 'being aggressive', 'opportunities for professional growth', 'high pay for good performance', and 'being competitive' as least characteristic of the organisation as he perceived it.

This was interesting to Steve, but to check that these weren't simply his own prejudices, he asked others with whom he worked closely to run through the items to see what they picked out. He found general agreement over the items. The one which they differed on was 'opportunities for professional growth'. Steve's colleagues felt that there were opportunities for growth and that Steve was wrong to relegate this item. On reflection, Steve rationalised this by realising that he had struggled for several years to get a promotion and had felt a bit disappointed to have waited so long. In retrospect, perhaps the promotion was coming at the right time, and he had grown and developed in his post.

As he went through the list, Steve had noted down a few items that, although not characteristic or uncharacteristic of the organisation, shed some light on the nature of his job. He noted attitudes to conflict. It wasn't that there was a low level of conflict or that people confronted it directly, but that people went out of their way to avoid conflict arising. He recalled the example of a manager who had been recruited recently but had left shortly afterwards. He seemed to favour a high conflict approach which led to all manner of trouble in a short space of time.

The above example illustrates two things. First, how to use the profile as a checklist to gain an understanding of your organisation's culture. Second, the importance of checking that your understanding of your organisation's culture is shared by others.

An integrated model of organisational entry analysis

■ ■ ■

77

You've probably noticed that analysis of the job and the organisational environment are not independent activities, and there are stages when it makes a lot of sense to combine them. How would you do this?

AN INTEGRATED MODEL FOR ORGANISATIONAL ENTRY ANALYSIS

1 Observe the job holder
 – the job
 – the environment
2 Structured interview with job holder
 – job analysis interview
 – organisational analysis interview
3 Critical incident analysis
4 Organisational analysis checklist
5 Interviews with those who interact with the job holder
 – job analysis
 – organisational analysis checklist

This is a logical approach to understanding the job and the environment in which it is set. The sequence begins with those tasks which will give you an overview of the job and its environment. This overview informs the later stages when you focus more critically on the key factors you identify. So, the sequence is a refining process that should produce an understanding that allows you to describe the job in detail and the key factors required for success.

You might find that you can omit some of the stages. The observation phase, for example, might be impractical because the job is so diverse that you couldn't hope to gain any sort of understanding of it in a short period of time.

Exercises for analysing a job

Earlier in this chapter, I asked you to identify a job that you wish to analyse; you can do this using the following series of activities. But before the activities, a word of caution. These days many people are concerned about job security. So, if you plan to analyse a job that isn't about to be filled, make sure the current job holder knows why you're analysing it; i.e. to help you understand organisational entry better.

The activities can be carried out separately or sequentially. You should look through them to see which you can do at the same sitting. For example, if time permits, your interviews could directly follow your observation.

Planning your analysis

Book some time with the current job holder, if there is one, to carry out your analysis. Explain to the job holder what a critical incident is, and ask them to try and think of examples in their own job; remember to explain why you are doing this.

Observing the job

Observe a person doing the job. Make notes on what you see, using the following headings as prompts.

- Tasks
- Skills
- Roles
- Environmental factors
- Interactions
- Working conditions
- Other factors

At the end of the observation ask the person how it felt to be observed, and how typical the observation period had been of their normal work. Make a note of how long the observation took.

Interviewing the hob holder

Look through the job analysis structured interview and edit out any unsuitable questions. Then talk to the job holder using the questions to structure your discussion.

Repeat the process, using the organisational analysis structural interview.

Critical incident analysis

Ask the job holder to recount a critical incident, including:

- the background and context of the incident
- what they actually did, or failed to do
- when the incident happened and when it might happen again.

Ask the job holder to recount as many critical incidents as they can remember.

Organisational analysis checklist

Show the job holder the organisational culture profile. Ask them which items are most and least characteristic of the organisation's culture. Then ask if any of the other items trigger any interesting insights about their job.

Interviewing other people

Arrange to meet the other people you need to speak to in order to get a full and complete understanding of the job. Run through the two structured interviews with them. Follow up with the critical incident analysis technique and the organisational culture profile.

Job descriptions
■ ■ ■

Now you've gathered all this information, you need to put it into some sort of order. You need to understand which points are the most important, for example, what are the key skills the job holder needs, what features of the culture will affect them, and also which aspects of the information are less important. Once you've done this, write up the job description and check it with the job holder; they'll usually find small errors and omissions at this stage which you will want to correct.

Job descriptions vary considerably, but good ones usually include most of the following:

- job title
- the position to which the job holder reports

- positions reporting to the job holder
- where the work is situated
- hours, grade and holidays
- goals and objectives
- tasks to be performed
- roles to be filled
- working conditions
- an indication of the organisation's culture.

This list is far from perfect. You need to tailor it to suit your own circumstances so that you end up with a document which reflects the job. A somewhat abbreviated example of a job description follows.

Job Title	Shift Manager
Grade:	R
Reports to:	Distribution Manager, Birmingham Warehouse
Reports:	Three supervisors and twenty staff
Location:	Birmingham Warehouse, Wednesbury
Hours:	Five 8-hour shifts per week
Holidays:	20 days (rising to 25) and bank holidays

Goals and Objectives
The efficient management of the clothing distribution line within budget. The full dispatch of all orders to customers' specifications.

Main Tasks and Responsibilities
- Responsible for the smooth running of the shift
- Co-ordinate and organise the staff on the shift
- Monitor the performance of staff on the shift
- Responsible for the condition of goods during the shift
- Report on shift to the manager of the following shift
- Introduce newcomers to their work
- Ensure that all staff have the required skills
- Organise training where needs exist
- Responsible for health and safety on shift
- Responsible for budget of approx. £800,000 p.a.

Working Environment
The job holder occupies a glass walled office on the shop floor which is shared with other shift managers. The environment in which the job is situated might be characterised as 'careful, attention is paid to detail, a low level of conflict exists, and a large amount of work is carried out in teams'. The shop floor is spotlessly clean, but noisy and draughty.

Other
The shift manager will be required to undertake such other duties as may be assigned by the Distribution Manager.

The purpose of job descriptions

A job description has three purposes:

- to check that you have properly understood the job
- to check that the job is a meaningful whole
- to describe the job to applicants.

The first of these points rather speaks for itself. But it's worth reiterating that you should show the job description to others to make sure that they agree with your assessment.

The second point refers back to Hackman and Oldham's model of job design. Is the job you've described 'complete'; will it motivate and satisfy the incumbent? To answer this question, you should check to see that the five core job characteristics are part of it. If not, then the person in the job is likely to perform poorly, and be less than fully motivated and satisfied. If you find that one or more of the core job dimensions are missing or weak, you should consider how you can rectify this. If this is not possible, you should be up front about it to applicants so that they can decide whether they want to pursue their interest. If you don't, they'll only find out when they start doing the job and that will again lead to dissatisfaction and lack of motivation.

81

The third point also rather speaks for itself. But I'd like to emphasise that your job description needs to be a true reflection of the job and not to romanticise it. If you make that mistake, you run the risk of raising false expectations and this will lead to considerable levels of dissatisfaction and lack of motivation, and might be another important contributing factor leading to the person leaving the organisation. The description of Steve's job is an example of a true reflection of the job.

Writing a job description

If you completed the activities earlier in the chapter, you will now have a lot of data about the job you want to analyse. The next thing to do is to put this data into some sort of order that demonstrates that you've fully understood the nature of the job; i.e. you need to produce a job description. Using the example, try to produce your own job description. When you have completed it, show it to the current job holder, or someone else who knows the job well, to see if it is an accurate representation of the job.

Selection criteria

■ ■ ■

You probably noticed that the example job description didn't contain all the information gleaned from the analysis. Why? Well, the main purpose of the analysis was to determine the criteria for selection, rather than to describe the job. It just so happened that some of the information gathered described the job, which in turn helped to check that the job was 'complete' and to describe it to applicants. Not all the information gathered would be relevant or appropriate to disclose to applicants as it might enable them to 'cheat' at the selection tests. However, this shouldn't be used as an excuse to limit the scope or detail of the job description. In most cases, the better informed applicants are, the better will be your decision making and applicants' levels of motivation should they join.

But it is a fact that not all the information gathered will appear in the job description and this explains the model of analysis I described earlier, which suggests that the selection criteria are formed from the raw data gathered during job and organisational analysis and the job description. If you just used the job description, you would be likely to miss many important factors leading to high performance and greater motivation and satisfaction.

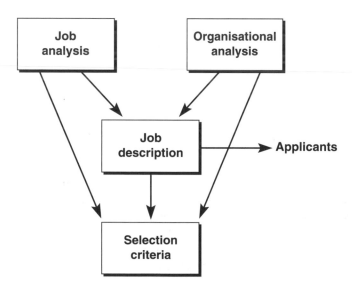

Fig 5.3 The organisational entry analysis process

In a rational approach to decision making, everything evolves from the development of the selection criteria. They provide the focus for organisational entry analysis and then act as justification for the choice of applicant. They can also be used to help with the choice of recruitment and selection methods and the planning of introduction and socialisation activities.

Qualities of selection criteria

If you have carried out organisational entry analysis you should have all the information you need to produce some selection criteria.

> **SELECTION CRITERIA are the knowledge, skills, abilities and other attributes (KSAOs) that a job holder needs in order to perform to a high standard, exert a lot of effort, and get satisfaction from the job. The selection criteria become apparent from the information gathered during organisational entry analysis.**
>
> **SELECTION CRITERIA must be:**
> - **job related**
> - **primary factors**
> - **achievable**
> - **measurable**
> - **distinguishable.**

83

Job related

Clearly, selection criteria need to be job related. However, job related means more than the skills and knowledge required to do the job; it includes factors related to the environment in which the job is set, which are so important for the motivation of the job holder.

Primary factors

Think about our warehouse manager for a moment. Clearly, the incumbent needs to be intelligent, and must be able to cope with the complexity in the job. But does this mean the particular number of 'O' levels or degree that would commonly appear on selection criteria? No, these are secondary issues. The primary factor is that the job holder must have a general level of intelligence that could have been developed in a number of ways. The selection criteria should not create artificial barriers which would exclude able applicants.

Achievable

Selection criteria often have a degree of aspiration in them – the perfect candidate is commonly described – but they are useless if it is not possible to achieve the items on the list. For example, this can easily happen when you want to find people with skills in a new computer package which no one in the world has yet gained. It's more common though for a combination of criteria to produce this effect, and it's important to check your completed selection criteria for this. Simply ask yourself whether the person exists, and would be likely to apply for the job.

Measurable

Every selection criterion must be measurable. If it is not, it is of no use to the selector. Where possible it should also be specific in the quantity or quality required. However, care needs to be taken here, as it isn't always possible to describe the quantity or quality required. For example, you might be particularly interested in a quality such as diplomacy, or the ability to prevent people related problems arising. It isn't practical or possible to explain exactly how much diplomacy is required. One approach to this problem is to break down the criterion to its constituent parts. So, for the ability to prevent people related problems arising, you might state that the person needs a qualification in management, experience in a similar managerial position, a first degree, and excellent interpersonal skills. But a person may possess all these qualities, yet still be completely unable to prevent people related problems emerging. In doing this you lose the vital complexity and interaction of factors that contribute to high performance. The sum of the parts isn't always greater than the whole.

The point I'm making here is that you want to bring to the surface the factors underpinning performance and satisfaction. These are often complex, and as such are not easily quantified. But they can be measured objectively via qualitative assessment. Careful questioning that aims to produce evidence regarding what the applicant values, what the applicant says they would do in particular circumstances (or have done in the past), their knowledge and so on is just as valuable and as objective as numerical data or yes/no answers. The difficulty often relates to the identification of evidence. This can come in all manner of ways: observation, recorded comments, inferences from what has been said and so on. As you go through the selection process you need to record these for future comparison of the applicant to the selection criteria.

When developing selection criteria you need to know *how* you will measure them, rather than how much the ability is required. A good way to check the usefulness of complex selection criteria is to think about possible questions that you could pose to applicants. Then think about the possible answers and how these could indicate that the person satisfies the criteria. If you cannot do this, don't include it in the selection criteria.

> **Your selection criteria need to capture the essence of success with all its complexity and interrelations, rather than relying on a simplistic approach that is unrealistic.**

Distinguishable

Each selection criterion should be distinct from the others. This helps to ensure that the attention of selectors is focused on the key elements and that the selection criteria capture the key primary factors. If you simply repeat the same criterion in different guises, all you do is give extra weight to that item which might be unwarranted. In addition, you need to determine which of the criteria are essential (i.e. an applicant *must* possess them before they could be offered a job) and which criteria are desirable (i.e. an applicant *should* possess before they could be offered a job). This is an important distinction to make because failure of an applicant to meet an essential criterion should automatically lead to that person's removal from the list of candidates. Clearly, it is important to check that all the criteria labelled as essential would produce this effect.

85

Developing selection criteria

The first stage of developing selection criteria is to gather your information together, examine it and establish the important KSAOs. These must be linked to the job and to either performance, motivation, or satisfaction. If they are related to one of these, then they are related to all the others. Ideally, you want to produce a list of between twenty and thirty items. Be careful not to produce items that are too general, such as 'must be able to type'. You will need to measure or test each of the criteria, so it would be better to say, 'must be able to type at least 55 words per minute'.

Once you've got your list of items, you examine them for fairness and suitability. For each one ask yourself, 'how do I justify the inclusion of this item in the selection criteria?' If it is appropriate, you should be able to give a brief justification that ties it into the job and explain how it helps the person perform better. Be careful not to include anything that would apply differently to different genders, races, or to married people. If in any doubt, don't include the item.

> ### How do I justify the inclusion of this item in the selection criteria?

It's unlikely that any applicant would be able to satisfy all the criteria, so now you need to decide upon some form of ranking. A useful framework places the criteria into four groups:

- essential criteria related to the job
- essential criteria related to the organisational environment
- desirable criteria related to the job
- desirable criteria related to the organisational environment.

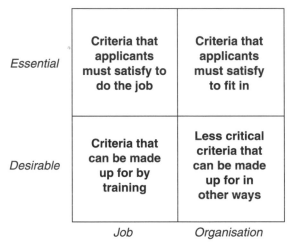

	Job	Organisation
Essential	Criteria that applicants must satisfy to do the job	Criteria that applicants must satisfy to fit in
Desirable	Criteria that can be made up for by training	Less critical criteria that can be made up for in other ways

Fig 5.4 The different types of selection criteria

Essential criteria are those that applicants must fulfil to be offered the job. So, you wouldn't include those KSAOs that realistic and available training could help a person to meet. If a person fails to meet any of the essential criteria they will automatically be eliminated. Obvious examples would include the need for a HGV licence for a HGV driver, or an ACA, ACCA, or ICMA qualification for a finance director. Although these can be developed, time constraints make training impractical and unrealistic.

The desirable criteria are all the other criteria that you consider important for success in the job. These do not produce 'critical failures', i.e. reasons for automatic elimination of a candidate, as there may be ways of making up for failure on any of them. However, for every one that an applicant fails to meet, you should be able to detail exactly how you will compensate for that failure. By adopting this model, you ensure that you only include those items that are important for success, and you also give yourself a framework for use later in the organisational entry process.

Earlier we saw how Steve, the warehouse shift manager, constructed a description of his job. The next stage is for Steve to design his selection criteria. To do this, he returned to the data he unearthed during his various efforts at analysis. He also looked again at the job description that he had produced. As he read through the material, it dawned on him that three factors were critical to his success. These were qualities that the job holder had to have to be able to do the job and that couldn't really be 'trained into' a new person. They were:

- the ability to avoid people related problems arising
- the diplomacy to manage the relationship with customers
- interpersonal skills and values suitable for the organisation.

He viewed these as primary level factors which encompassed a number of subsidiary issues. He felt that they were essential. He also knew that he would be able to find people with these skills. His only problem was to specify how to measure each one.

The ability to prevent people related problems arising
How could Steve quantify this? He realised that his ability to run a troublefree shift could be measured by some of his output targets: percentage of customer orders dispatched on schedule, number of failures, number of complaints, levels of staff satisfaction, and so on. Such measures could be applied to anyone managing people in a commercial environment. As Steve pondered this, several interview questions occurred to him 'how can you measure staff satisfaction?' 'how do you prioritise work in the department?' 'what would cause you to change work priorities during a shift?' 'how do you balance the needs of the customer and your own company?' and so on. He noted these questions and developed a clear idea of answers that would demonstrate that the applicant satisfied the criterion. He decided to leave the measurement of this criterion a little open so that he wouldn't be inherently biased against applicants from outside a distribution environment who might measure this type of effectiveness in another way. However, that didn't stop Steve developing some sharp questions that he would want to put to applicants on this subject.

The diplomacy to manage relationships with customers

Steve thought that this criterion would be a little easier to measure than the previous one. First, he wanted evidence that the applicants had been in regular contact with external customers. He would then ask them to describe examples of this interaction and typical problems that might occur. He also decided to develop some hypothetical questions from his own experience to test how applicants would react. He would have a predetermined marking scheme to grade applicants' answers.

Interpersonal skills and values suitable for the organisation

Steve knew that these were essential for high performance in the job. Every manager had to be able to communicate with people at all levels of the organisation and to adopt appropriate behaviour. In his analysis he had developed an understanding of attitudes towards conflict and teamworking and also the formal nature of relationships in the organisation. He decided that careful questioning on these topics would help him determine how well applicants fitted in.

Desirable criteria

Steve identified a number of other criteria which, although important, were not critical and could be made up for in other ways. They included:

- the ability to plan and co-ordinate staffing activities
- the ability to train people to perform particular tasks
- common sense
- knowledge of the operation.

In addition to these, Steve identified two supplementary factors which, though important, could easily be accommodated in other ways:

- report writing
- health and safety certification.

All these desirable criteria were measurable through structured interview questions or other selection tests, although it was impossible to determine the actual levels of each which would be required.

Essential criteria

1. *The ability to prevent people related problems arising*
Applicants must be able to demonstrate experience and the ability to manage people in an operational environment where they have had to organise the work of others. They should be able to recount examples of situations where they have prevented problems arising.

2. *The ability to manage relationships with customers*
Applicants must be able to demonstrate that they have, or could, work in a managerial position in direct contact with external customers without detrimentally affecting the relationship between the two companies. They should be able to recount examples of their own actions which have helped the relationship between the two parties.

3. *Interpersonal skills and values suitable for the company*
Applicants must be able to 'fit in' with existing values and modes of behaviour within the organisation. In particular, applicants must value teamwork, low levels of conflict and be able to work in an environment with a high degree of regulation. Applicants will demonstrate this by analysing how they respond to different types of organisational environment.

Desirable criteria
1. The ability to plan and co-ordinate staffing activities
2. The ability to train people to perform particular tasks
3. Common sense
4. Knowledge of the operation

Supplementary criteria
1. Report writing skills
2. Certification in health and safety

89

An extract from the selection criteria for a shift manager

This example is a short extract from the selection criteria that Steve would have produced for the job of shift manager in a distribution warehouse. Its format isolates the key skills and abilities that any applicant must have to be effective in the job. It also indicates how these will be measured.

If you've been involved in much organisational entry, these selection criteria will probably look quite unusual. They are much more discursive than normal; this is deliberate. The underlying qualities required to be effective in a position are rarely defined easily with reference to a couple of qualifications and some experience. They need to be more subtle and to demonstrate the complexity of the work. The purpose of the analysis phase of organisational entry is to discover the key factors contributing to an employee's effectiveness, not to generate an endless list of almost meaningless and irrelevant items that are only vaguely connected to the job. For example, this specification could easily include five years experience of working in a distribution warehouse, three 'A' levels, qualification from the Institute of Purchasing and Supply, and so on. Whilst all of these things might be useful, it's just as likely that someone will apply without these qualifications who could do the job very well. You need to understand why someone needs these qualifications, and that's what the selection criteria described earlier try to do.

Producing selection criteria

Now that you've analysed the job and produced a job description, you're in a position to produce the all-important selection criteria. What are the factors in the job critical to performance? Try to produce selection criteria for the job you've been analysing.

When you've done this, check back over the relevant section of this chapter to see whether your criteria have the characteristics of good criteria. Also, show your list to people in your organisation who can determine whether it is accurate and realistic.

Applicant initiated criteria

There is a fifth type of criteria that often plays an important part in the decision to recruit someone. These are initiated by applicants and are factors you consider important which were not in the original selection criteria. These new factors might reshape the priority of your existing selection criteria or introduce completely new ones. These can be very powerful in influencing your decision. For example, an interviewee for Steve's job might talk about a new way of dispatching orders that the company doesn't currently use. Such ideas can make the applicant seem very attractive indeed.

How do you handle such criteria? The only way is to try to recognise these factors after you've met someone. Write them down and analyse them. For example, knowledge of new distribution systems is admirable, but can the techniques be used in the company? If not, how will this affect the motivation of the new recruit? All you can do is to be aware of applicant initiated criteria, record and then analyse them. Ask yourself 'how relevant is this new criterion to the job?'.

Change analysis
■ ■ ■

> Organisational entry decisions greatly affect existing employees. You must think about how the recruitment of a new member of staff will change the jobs, aspirations and expectations of others.

All organisational entry matters are concerned with the management of change. Whether it be a reorganisation of existing members of staff, job redesign, or the selection of an external candidate, significant changes will affect many people. Issues such as how those people passed over for promotion react, how existing members of staff will get on with a newcomer, and how work is redistributed will critically affect the performance of the team. You should take steps to analyse the impact that your decisions will have on other people.

Analysing change

91

Change is a very large subject which could easily fill this book. It is not possible to do full justice to the subject. Instead, I want to look at a series of questions you can use to analyse the change you are planning to make when introducing a new member of staff to the organisation. In doing so, I shall concentrate on the reactions of existing members of staff, as it is these people who are most likely to be affected by the change.

How will the newcomer affect existing workers?

Think about the post you're trying to fill and work through the following questions.

- Describe the situation you want to change.
- Why is this change necessary?
- What is the exact nature of the change?
- How will the change affect people?
- Who is affected by it?
- What do they stand to lose?
- How can they gain from the change?
- What are the implications of the change to them?
- How will they react to these implications?
- Would people resist the change?
- How could they resist it?
- What strategies can you use to minimise resistance to the change?

SUMMARY – CHAPTER 5 *ANALYSIS*

- Mistakes during the analysis stage of organisational at entry cascade down through the whole process.

- If you don't know what you're looking for, how can you expect to find it?

- Job analysis looks at:
  - the tasks that must be accomplished
  - the skills required to do the work
  - the roles that are held.

- Observing a job gives you an overview of it.

- Structured interviews with current and past job holders help you get a fuller understanding of the position.

- You must analyse and design new as well as existing jobs.

- Organisational fit analysis is the process of identifying the important factors in the environment that contribute towards high levels of performance and satisfaction.

- When analysing the environmental factors affecting a person at work, you need to understand:
  - interactions with other people
  - reward systems
  - values
  - organisation-wide initiatives
  - working conditions
  - psychological contracts.

- Job descriptions are used to:
  - check that you have properly understood the job
  - check that the job is a meaningful whole
  - describe the job to applicants.

- Selection criteria are used to:
  - determine what recruitment methods are likely to attract suitably qualified applicants
  - choose appropriate selection techniques
  - decide which applicant best fits the job and the culture.

6

■ ■ ■

How do you attract applicants?

CHAPTER OBJECTIVES

After reading this chapter you should be able to:
- describe the purpose of recruitment
- explain how recruitment works
- design a recruitment programme
- write an effective job advertisement
- attract suitably qualified people
- manage the relationship with an external consultant
- describe how you will treat internal applicants.

CHAPTER OVERVIEW

In this chapter, I look at how you can attract a pool of applicants for a vacancy. I suggest that it is important to attract a small number of suitably qualified applicants so that you can give every applicant your full attention. To do this, you need to be able to segment the job market and target your advertising. I show you how to do this and how to write an appropriate job advertisement. On many occasions it is preferable to use a third party to manage the process of attracting applicants; this is a relationship that must be professionally managed. Finally, I ask whether internal and external applicants are different and should be treated differently.

The purpose of recruitment
■ ■ ■

There's a famous old book called *Parkinson's Law* in which C. Northcote Parkinson humorously describes various historical approaches to the attraction of applicants. He concludes that the reason why selection fails 'is mainly due to there being too many candidates'. If you have too many candidates – all of whom fill in the requisite forms, have the required level of experience, quote three admirable referees etc. – how on earth can you do them all justice and distinguish between them? In reality, most people who apply for most jobs could do the job to a reasonable standard with a little training. Advertisements that attract hundreds, or even thousands of applicants simply serve to mask the better candidates, increase the expense of the process, and make it 'pot luck' as to who is finally selected. As Parkinson says, 'it would have saved time and trouble to do some thinking in the first place'.

We have come to think that more is better in recruitment, but Parkinson (and common sense) suggest that this isn't the case. If the purpose of recruitment isn't to attract a large number of applicants, what is its purpose?

> **The purpose of recruitment is to attract a small number of highly suitable applicants.**

This has a number of advantages:

- the administration is simpler and cheaper
- it is more likely that you will identify the best applicant
- you do not waste the time, and raise the expectations, of others who are unlikely to be offered the job.

How do you ensure that you only attract applications from a small number of highly suitable candidates?

- Communicate the fact that a vacancy exists somewhere that is likely to be seen by your target market.
- Detail the skills, abilities, experience, values etc. you want to attract.
- Describe exactly what you expect from the person.
- Describe the environment in which the job is situated.
- Describe what you have to offer the employee.

These items need to be described accurately so that applicants can realistically determine whether they have the skills and abilities you need, whether or not they can enjoy working in the environment, and whether the rewards are sufficient. In short, you need to give potential applicants the information they need to determine whether or not the job would be right for them. This information can be conveyed in advertisements, further details, job descriptions, brochures or some other media.

Realistic recruitment

There is a golden rule of recruitment: give a realistic picture of the job and the organisation to potential applicants. If you 'dress it up', you will raise expectations that cannot be met during employment. This will lead to resentment, dissatisfaction, lack of commitment and, ultimately, the decision to leave the company.

> **The golden rule of recruitment: *'tell it like it is'.***

95

What are realistic job previews

The best way to 'tell it like it is' is to give applicants the opportunity to do the job for a while. This helps them to decide whether it is a job they can do well and whether or not they'll be able to cope with the environment. Research has shown that realistic job previews reduce staff turnover and increase satisfaction.

A REALISTIC JOB PREVIEW IN A FAST-FOOD RESTAURANT

Jean   'Liam, we were impressed with you on Monday. Are you still interested in the trainee manager's job?'

Liam   'Very much.'

Jean   'We'd like you to come along for an 'on-the-job experience'. Is that OK?'

Liam   'Sure. What does it involve?'

Jean   'We'd like you spend a couple of days as a crew member. You'll serve customers, clean the store, count stock, cook and so on. All the jobs you'll do if you get the job. We'll also ask you to have a go at a few tests.'

Liam   'Fine. Where and when?'

Jean   'Next Tuesday and Wednesday. That's the 11th and 12th of February. Tuesday from 10 am 'til 6 pm, and from 4 pm 'til 2 am on Wednesday. That'll be at our Coleraine restaurant in the High Street. Ask for Andy Beattie when you arrive.'

A week later

Noel   'What was it like?'

Liam   'It's a joke. I spent hours standing with no break. Those restaurants get hot you know. And there's a constant stream of customers – it never stops. The other staff seem to know their jobs and that makes you look incompetent. I was knackered after a couple of hours. And then, right at the end, at one o'clock in the morning, they made me count stock in the freezer. It was minus 20 in there. There was snow on the ground outside. I didn't get home 'til 2.30. Heaven knows who can do that job.'

96

This example is a fictional rendering of an actual realistic job preview at a leading fast-food restaurant. Liam's comments reflect one potential trainee manager's feelings about the preview. The company can justify its actions because it gives applicants a very accurate preview of what their job will be like. As it takes school leavers and graduates into its trainee management programme, the realistic job preview is particularly important.

Do realistic job previews work?

As Liam was given such a realistic preview of the manager's job in a fast-food restaurant, why do you think he accepted it only to leave within a year?

This example illustrates one of the greatest problems in organisational entry: the problem of supply and demand and the fact that many people see a new job as salvation from their current employer or the dole queue. In this case, Liam was so desperate for work that he was prepared to do virtually anything to start his managerial career.

Realistic job previews are usually used in one of two ways:

- to reduce inflated expectations
- to inflate depressed expectations.

There are many different ways to show applicants what the job is really like. The most realistic, of course, is to ask applicants to do the job. But often this is not practical. So organisations have developed a number of other methods. These include:

- brochures and booklets
- site visits
- the opportunity to talk freely with members of the organisation who are not involved in the selection decision
- narrated slide presentations
- oral presentations
- videos.

Designing realistic job previews

The leading researcher and writer on realistic job previews, John Wanous, suggests six guidelines:

- **encourage self-selection explicitly** – tell applicants the purpose of the realistic job preview, i.e. to decide whether or not the job is right for them
- **the message must be credible**
- **the medium and the message must be consistent** – for example, don't include pictures of people smiling when you're communicating a negative message
- **communicate feelings as well as information**
- **mirror organisational climates** – communicate the 'good news' as well as the 'bad news'
- **do the preview early.**

Could you give applicants a realistic preview of the job?

Think about the job that you want to fill. How could you give someone a realistic preview of it? Read through the types of previews that organisations use which were described a little earlier. If that isn't helpful, use Wanous' model to design your own realistic job preview.

Given the range of jobs that you might be seeking to fill, it is impossible to guess which realistic recruitment techniques you might have chosen or, possibly, developed. Often it can be quite difficult to incorporate these techniques into your organisational entry process. However, the benefits have been shown to be substantial and reduce staff dissatisfaction and turnover. They work because people begin work with their eyes open, fully aware of what is expected of them.

How does recruitment attract people?

You might think this an odd question to ask. But before we can think about the best methods to attract applicants, we need to know how advertising actually works. How does it affect people? How does it encourage people to put pen to paper and send in an application form or CV? There are two views on the subject, each of which is known by an acronym: AIDA and ATR.

AIDA

Awareness ➜ Interest ➜ Desire ➜ Action

The idea is that an advertisement raises awareness which induces an interest. This interest is translated into a desire for the post which, in turn, stimulates the action of applying for the job. In a perfect world, job advertisements would always work because they would stimulate interest in this way. So you would only have interested people applying for the job. Unfortunately, this isn't always the case.

ATR

Awareness ➜ Trial ➜ Reinforcement

ATR differs from AIDA in that the raised awareness translates itself directly into trial. Reinforcement, or the development of interest, comes after the application has been made. This is important because many people have prepared CVs which they send to every vacancy that might be appropriate. People who respond in this way make your job much more difficult and time-consuming. It's not that they aren't potentially very good employees, but that thoughtless applications increase the volume without necessarily increasing the quality. To combat this problem, you need to make the requirements explicit in your advertisement so that the 'bulk responder' can determine quickly and easily whether the job is suitable for them.

Should you incorporate corporate advertising?

Increasingly, advertisements for jobs carry supplementary information about the organisation. Sometimes this is to help the potential applicant decide whether it's an organisation they'd like to work for. But, more often than not, the purpose of the advertising is to promote the company. When a job advertisement is placed in a trade journal, the organisation knows that it will be read by other players in the industry. As such, it is likely to have an important role in positioning the firm. However, when corporate advertising is included in a job advertisement, there is a danger of a conflict of interest. The person reading it needs to be able to determine whether or not the job is right for them, whether they will be able to enjoy working in the particular organisation. Corporate advertising often portrays an organisation in a very positive light, one which might be unrecognisable to someone who works there. This can be dangerous as an applicant believing this message will join the organisation with expectations that simply cannot be met.

Do you attract applicants yourself?

This is the first question that you must ask yourself. Do I attract applicants myself, or should I contract out the process to a third party? It is not an easy question to answer. And managerial judgement is the most important tool you have to help you decide. There are several factors you should take into account.

Time   How quickly do you really need to find someone? Carrying out recruitment yourself is usually quicker than briefing a third party. However, the quickest method of all is to use an agency, if they have the type of people you require. Temp agencies, for example, can sometimes have someone for you within the hour.

99

Cost   Using a third party usually incurs a cost. However, before dismissing third parties out of hand because of the cost, take into account the hidden costs you will incur by carrying out recruitment yourself. Your staff's and your time is a cost. If you place an advertisement, you are unlikely to achieve the rates that an external consultant can achieve due to volume buying. And the biggest cost of all is failing to find the best person possible.

Administration   Third party recruitment transfers much of the administration of the process to the consultant. You probably want to send one or two letters to every applicant. This consumes much secretarial time. How many applications have you got the capacity to administer?

Location of suitable applicants   Do you know where you are likely to find suitable applicants? Some third party recruitment consultants have specialist knowledge of an industry, profession, or location.

Approaching suitable applicants   Sometimes you need to approach applicants directly. In your industry it might, or might not, be ethical for one company to approach a competitor's employees directly. When you are unable to do this, headhunters will undertake the work for you and separate you from the direct approach.

Level and type of job Recruitment abounds with tradition. Several levels and types of jobs require a particular manner of approach. Applicants for very senior or very specialised jobs, for example, are commonly best attracted through headhunters who can pander to egos.

Company policy Does your organisation have a policy regarding recruitment strategies?

Should you use an external consultant?

- How quickly do you need to find a new recruit?
- How much can you spend attracting new recruits?
- How many applications can you administer internally?
- Do you know where you are likely to find suitable applicants?
- Are you able to approach all suitable applicants directly?
- Does the level or type of vacancy shape your decision?
- What company policy must you take into account?

100

Review your answers. Do any of the above questions force you to adopt a particular style of recruitment?

Attracting applicants yourself

■ ■ ■

If you decide to attract applicants yourself, there are several things you must think about:

- administration
- the legal aspects of recruitment
- designing a recruitment strategy.

Administration

One of the hidden costs of organisational entry is the administration. These hidden costs can quickly and invisibly creep up on you. Imagine that you place an advertisement that has attracted two hundred replies. What administrative difficulties does this create?

- Do you want applicants to fill out application forms?
- Will you send out application forms?
- Will you send out further particulars and a job description?
- Will you acknowledge completed applications?
- Will you write to people to inform them of a negative outcome?

Several forms of cost are incurred in the above:

- printing
- postage
- stationery
- staff.

These quickly mount up, and it might easily cost £1000 to reply professionally to 200 applicants. Not surprisingly, many organisations have decided to treat applicants callously and do not acknowledge applications or inform applicants of negative decisions. You must decide what your approach will be. It is worth remembering that a lot of time, effort and trouble goes into every application, and for applicants every application is a psychological investment. As many people apply within industries, or to companies they admire, the way you handle applications will often have an impact on current or potential customers.

Application forms

101

Do you want to design or use your own application form? The big advantage of using your own application form is that you can incorporate factors from your selection criteria that will help you to narrow down the applicants on factors you know to be relevant to performance in the job. Another advantage is that you can more easily monitor the racial mix of applicants, as you can include appropriate questions.

Application forms have several disadvantages:

- the requirement to fill one in will reduce the number of applications you receive
- designing, printing and circulating them adds time and expense to the recruitment process.

Further particulars

In the previous chapter, I said that one of the purposes of job descriptions is to inform applicants about the nature of the job. In many circumstances, job descriptions are abbreviated and fail to convey a complete impression. As a result, you might want to supplement your job description with further particulars about the job, the organisation and, perhaps, its location. All these will help applicants determine whether their interest in the vacancy is genuine. Remember, it is important that applicants gain as thorough and accurate an impression about the job and organisation as possible.

Advertisements and the law

I covered the legal aspects of organisational entry in chapter 2. I stated that while you must select fairly, you may take positive action during the recruitment phase. Although the publicity of a vacancy must not contain anything that might be construed as discriminatory against a gender, racial group, or married people, you can choose to place **some** of your publicity material in media likely to attract the attention of under-represented groups. But you mustn't place all your publicity material in media that only people from particular minorities will see.

Designing a recruitment strategy

If you decide to attract applicants yourself, how do you decide which recruitment methods to use? The answer lies within your selection criteria. As your selection criteria contain a list of the essential and desirable qualities that applicants should have, they can be used to work out where people with these qualities might be. Once you know this, it should be relatively easy to devise a plan to attract their attention. But this is a little general to be of practical use. How do you actually go about targeting your market?

Targeting your market

Stage 1: Identifying the market segments

> A recruitment market segment is a group of potential applicants who all fulfil the essential selection criteria and who hold a common characteristic which is relevant in explaining and predicting their response to your approaches.

What does this definition mean? Firstly, it stresses the point that you only want to contact those people who satisfy the essential points laid out in the selection criteria. Secondly, it identifies that people satisfying the essential selection criteria can be grouped together in various ways. Thirdly, the separation of common characteristics helps you to understand better how you can make your publicity material more attractive to the segment. Finally, it suggests that you can predict how potential applicants will react to your publicity material based on a common characteristic.

So, a recruitment market segment is a group of people who each satisfy the essential characteristic and who share something in common. The following exercise looks at this definition in more depth.

What is a market segment?

In the previous chapter, I looked at the case of Steve, the distribution warehouse shift manager. I highlighted three essential selection criteria:

● the ability to avoid people related problems arising
● the diplomacy to manage the relationship with customers
● interpersonal skills and values suitable for the organisation.

Can you think of three groups of people likely to contain a significant number of people who satisfy these three points? What is the common characteristic of each of these groups?

The more obvious market segments are:

● *current employees in supervisory or managerial positions*
● *managers in similar positions in other distribution warehouses*
● *management consultants and temporary staff who specialise in solving distribution management problems*
● *members of racial groups under-represented in the organisation who have the relevant diplomacy and problem solving skills*
● *project managers in direct contact with customers*
● *production controllers in direct contact with customers.*

The first three of these groups are quite specific market segments. You've probably started to think how you could publicise the vacancy to each segment.

Stage 2: Understanding the market segments

Now that you've identified your market segments, the next stage is to understand them a little better. To be of use, a market segment should exhibit the following characteristics:

■ **measurability** – you should be able to determine how large the segment is and where it is to be found
■ **substantiality** – the segments you target should be large enough to warrant the amount of money you need to spend to penetrate them
■ **accessibility** – you must be able to reach the people in the segment

- **actionability** – you must be able to develop a plan to contact and respond to the segment.

> **Recruitment market segments must be:**
> 1 measurable
> 2 substantial
> 3 accessible
> 4 actionable.

Stage 3: Deciding which market segments to target

Once you've established a list of market segments that satisfy the four criteria – measurability, substantiality, accessibility, actionability – you need to rank them and determine which you wish to target. You need to target sufficient segments to give you an appropriate number of suitable applicants.

For each segment that you've identified, you need to establish the best method of attracting the attention of suitable people. Later in this chapter, I'll run through the possible recruitment methods available to you with a short discussion of the strengths and weaknesses of each. You need to get a feel for how many suitable applicants each method would produce. From that, and knowing the cost of the method, you can work out a simple 'cost per suitable applicant figure'. Your managerial judgement will tell you which segments to go for and how much to spend.

Where are your market segments?

Think about the position you wish to fill.

- What market segments can you identify?
- What are the common characteristics of the people in each segment that you can use to target publicity material?
- Are the segments viable?

  - Measurable
  - Substantial
  - Accessible
  - Actionable

- Which segments are worth approaching?
- What is the best way to approach each of the viable segments?

Methods of recruitment

Internal candidates

Most jobs are filled by internal candidates. This isn't surprising when you consider that internal applicants generally possess some important positive characteristics:

- past performance is known
- training requirements are known
- they understand, and have adapted to, the organisation's culture
- they have worked with the organisation's systems and processes
- they have working relationships and networks established.

There are few disadvantages associated with internal candidates assuming, of course, that they are the equal of external candidates. One disadvantage worth mentioning is that if you constantly recruit from within you may prevent new ideas and new ways of doing things from entering the organisation. This, however, is more theoretical than proven as there are no reasons why internal candidates cannot develop and expand in the same way as people working in other organisations. In addition, the transfer of ideas from other organisations is just as likely to be destructive as constructive.

How do you tell your employees that a vacancy exists? There are as many methods as organisations. Among the more common are:

- noticeboards
- newsletters
- team briefings
- appraisals
- EMail circulars
- memos
- enquires to the personnel department
- direct approaches.

In addition, the office grapevine will let many know of the vacancy. These methods benefit from being relatively cheap and quick to produce. By their own rules, some organisations must advertise jobs externally and cannot inform internal candidates of the vacancy – they must see the advertisement and respond to it. Does your organisation have a similar rule?

What methods can you use to advertise the job to internal candidates?

- List the methods that you could use to advertise a job internally. What coverage would each method achieve?
- Would these methods bring the vacancy to the attention of everyone you want?

Radio and television

Radio and television are used for recruitment. We tend to think of national advertisements for the regular or territorial army. But there are several other ways to use these media. Some independent television regions have special 'job hunters' programmes or time on Teletext. Radio catchment areas often mirror reasonable journey times to large towns or cities and are not as expensive as you might think. However, these media aren't used very often for some good reasons:

- radio and television are blunt instruments that are expensive when you calculate effective coverage (i.e. number of potential suitable applicants reached divided by total number of receivers of message multiplied by the cost per listener)
- being blunt instruments, they offer no market differentiation and no guarantee that the people you want to hear or see the advertisement will do so
- they tend to increase the number of applicants but not their quality or suitability
- they take time and money to produce.

Agencies

There are many different types of agencies that you can approach for applicants. The most well known are Job Centres or Employment Service. These will advertise your vacancy free of charge and have a vested interest in making it known to people looking for work. Job Centres are particularly useful when you are looking for unskilled or semiskilled staff. They are less useful, but worth investigating, for skilled, professional or managerial posts. Their big drawback is that only unemployed people are likely to see your advertisements.

Most other agencies have some form of specialisation or unique selling point. For example, some specialise in particular occupations – secretarial, accounting, catering, acting, computers etc. – or in particular regions, or a combination of both. Most commercial agencies will charge you a fee if you recruit one of the people they have introduced to you. There are other agencies that rarely charge a fee. These are outplacement services: commercial firms which usually collect their fees from the organisation dispensing with staff. They add to their reputation if they can place staff with organisations. There are also several outplacement agencies for the armed services. The 'peace dividend' has reduced the size of the armed forces. Consequently, there are many well trained, professional staff (both managerial and non-managerial) looking for work in the commercial environment. The armed forces have always trained their people well and, as a result, armed forces outplacement agencies can be excellent places to look for skilled staff.

Agencies have two big advantages:

- **speed** – if they have the people you require, you can be interviewing the same day
- **specificity** – you can be very tight in your requirements 'I need someone who can type at 60 wpm, speaks fluent Japanese, and lives within easy commuting distance of Islington'.

There are drawbacks, of course. These include:

- **expense** – agencies fees vary, but they are not cheap
- **suitability** – there may not be an agency that you can refer to for help with your type of vacancy
- **blankness** – agencies are of no use to you if they don't have a person with the skills and abilities you require on their books
- **additional contacts** – once you speak to some agencies, you're on their mailing and call lists for life (which can be more annoying than double glazing salespeople phoning you at home in the evening).

Employee referral programmes

Recruitment can be a costly process. Whether it's fees to agents or consultants, advertising space, or simply the costs of administration, costs quickly mount. To reduce such costs, many organisations have introduced employee referral schemes. These schemes offer a reward, commonly about £500, to any employee who introduces a new recruit to the organisation. Whilst these schemes reduce costs and introduce people who are better aware of the organisation's culture than other applicants, it's simply a matter of luck whether you will find suitable applicants for your vacancy.

Direct approaches

Speculative, direct approaches by people to organisations are more successful than you might imagine. Why? Well, one reason seems to be that speculative approaches are well researched. So, they are often from people who know what they can offer your organisation and why you should employ them. A good human resources or personnel department will keep a record of people who have written to your organisation. Unfortunately, such is the success of this job seeking strategy that many outplacement and recruitment agencies circulate lists of organisations for their clients to merge letters to. This somewhat reduces the likelihood of you finding well researched speculative applications. Nevertheless, this can be a rich source of strong applicants.

Temporary to regular

This little known method of recruitment is actually one of the best around. The idea is that you fill a vacancy with a temporary member of staff (either on a short term contract with the organisation or through an agency) as a way of seeing whether the person is suitable for permanent employment. The benefits of this type of recruitment include:

- you can observe how well suited the person is to the job
- you can observe how well suited the person is to the organisation and the people with whom they interact
- you can spot potential
- it lets either side walk away from the relationship with little harm to either party
- speed.

However, there are drawbacks and limitations to this recruitment method:

- it is only suitable for the types of jobs where temporary labour is commonly used
- agencies will charge a hefty fee if you recruit their temporary staff and might take umbrage and not supply you with temporary staff in future
- it might cause you to be seen as a callous recruiter as accusations might circulate about you being a 'hire 'em, fire 'em' employer
- as temporary staff commonly have higher wages than regular staff and are paid by the hour with generous overtime rates, converting them to regular staff might meet with resistance or lead to dissatisfaction
- it might be impractical because the people you want are currently working on permanent contracts and won't take the risk of leaving for a temporary contract
- temporary staff might treasure their independence and not want to switch to permanent contracts.

Posters

Posters can be a very effective method of recruitment. Perhaps the most common usage is by retailers looking for shop staff. They work well when you want to recruit staff from a specific location, when your staff are likely to come from the same target market as your customers, or when you are looking for casual or unskilled people. But posters suffer the drawbacks of blunt instruments already discussed.

Schools and colleges

Do you want to recruit someone who hasn't been influenced by working in other organisations? If so, then schools and colleges are a natural place to look for staff. Most schools and colleges have careers sections that are only too keen to receive advances from organisations offering jobs. The advantages of recruiting from educational establishments are fairly obvious:

- labour costs are low
- there are many people needing work

109

- you can recruit the managers of tomorrow and immerse them in the organisation's ways of doing things
- you can greatly influence attitudes to work
- they can be useful for particular skills (multiple languages, nuclear physicists, research scientists etc.)
- energy levels are high.

However, recruiting from such establishments does have its limitations:

- most staff will be unskilled
- training costs will be high
- initial promise may not always be forthcoming
- there is a high turnover of new recruits in their first job
- there are only several 'windows' each year when you can take on people.

Job fairs

Job fairs are very effective methods of recruitment that are frequently overlooked by managers. People who attend job fairs range from unskilled workers looking for casual work right up to chief executives. They also attract people in work who are simply curious about the job market or their value. Job fairs work best when your organisation has a number of posts to fill as you maximise your investment. The main benefits are:

- you can fill vacancies quickly as you might complete recruitment and selection at the same time
- you can fill future vacancies
- the cost of each new recruit can be quite low
- you get wider exposure for your organisation.

However, very few companies use job fairs. Why? There seem to be several reasons:

- not many managers know about job fairs or how to participate in them
- although cheap to enter, there are costs in setting up and staffing a stand
- there might not always be a job fair around when you want to recruit
- there is no guarantee how effectively the job fair will be marketed.

Newspaper advertisements

When most people decide to attract applicants themselves their immediate thought is 'let's run an ad'. And for very good reason. Newspaper advertisements:

- will be seen be many people
- are easy to produce
- get a reasonably quick response
- are the traditional way of attracting people.

In cities in particular, local newspapers (and free job magazines) carry pages of vacancies covering all levels and types of jobs. The 'Sundays' carry more exclusive job advertisements usually geared to a particular market niche. Anyone looking for work is almost certain to read through the advertisements in the relevant newspaper, journal or magazine. Despite this, such advertisements should not be an automatic choice as there are some serious drawbacks to advertising:

- they can be very expensive, especially when you repeat them
- they are a 'shot gun' approach relying on broad coverage rather than on a better targeted approach
- they are only seen by people actively looking for work
- response rates drop markedly the more specialised the advertisement becomes
- poorly defined advertisements can attract huge numbers of replies that are costly to respond to and difficult to filter

- advertisements rarely communicate the true nature of the job well
- results are inconsistent – what do you do if no one replies?

Nevertheless, despite the potential drawbacks you should always consider advertisements as a method of attracting applicants. When successful, they are quick, simple and reasonably cost effective.

Where could you advertise your job?

- If you were to recruit someone to do your own job, where would you place advertisements?
- How many applicants do you think you would attract?
- Would you get enough suitable applicants?

Designing a newspaper advertisement

Given that recruitment through advertisements is so popular and universal, I should quickly describe how you go about writing a good advertisement.

Stage 1: Understand the market   The first stage is to develop an understanding of the segments of the market you wish to target. This subject was covered a little earlier.

Stage 2: Evaluate the media   Once you're sure you understand people in the segments that you wish to attract, the next stage is to find out which media are most likely to reach them. You can ask several questions to narrow down your choice of media:

- Is your target audience working or out of work?

If it is in work, the trade press is likely to be particularly useful if, of course, there is a relevant trade press. The more general press is usually better if the audience is out of work.

- Is there a traditional way of attracting the attention of your segment?

There are several professions – secretarial, accountancy etc. – that a whole recruitment industry has built up around. There are many specialist free journals that advertise such jobs.

- Is there a magazine market serving the segment in which jobs are advertised?

This might seem an obvious question to ask, but it frequently gets forgotten. Magazine advertisements have the advantage of being seen by the casual reader who might not be actively looking for a job, but who becomes interested in your vacancy.

- Do you want to attract the interest of any groups that are under-represented in your organisation?

As I said earlier, it is perfectly legal to place advertisements in media likely to be seen by an under-represented group. The only rule is that your advertising mustn't only be placed in such media.

- What is the coverage rate (or readership) of the media you are interested in?

This is important because you want to be sure that the media you choose will actually reach your segment.

- What is the cost of the space for your advertisement?

An obvious concern which can affect your choice of media when combined with information on coverage rates.

- How many responses do you want?

It isn't uncommon for advertisements in the national press to receive tens of thousands of replies. Such a response could swamp your ability to handle the administration and lead to needless cost. You should investigate typical response rates for the media you might use.

- Must your advertisement serve a dual purpose and also advertise the organisation?

I would strongly recommend against this dual purpose of job advertisements as it tends to boost response rates with no improvement in quality. This leads to additional administrative costs. If you have to include corporate advertising then this can dictate the placement of your advertisement, for example, in a certain magazine so that the industry see it. If you do this you should check to ensure that your advertisement will still be seen by people in your target segment.

Stage 3: Writing the advertisement There are two types of message you should convey:

1. *Realistic messages.* The purpose of realistic messages is to 'tell it like it is' including positive and negative aspects of the job and working in the organisation. By conveying a realistic message, you help potential applicants determine whether or not they are genuinely interested in the position. The idea behind the realistic message is that new recruits join informed about the job and the organisation, and with realistic expectations about work. As a result, newcomers are less likely to be disappointed by false expectations and be more motivated and more likely to stay.

2. *Targeted messages.* As you might have gathered from the tone of the chapter so far, I also favour targeted messages in job advertisements that speak directly to people in specific market segments. Targeted messages should also be realistic messages. Such messages will help to ensure that those who respond to your advertisements are genuinely interested in the vacancy and more likely to meet the selection criteria. Additionally, by managing expectations, newcomers are likely to have the enhanced levels of motivation etc. mentioned above.

If you have identified two or more segments that you wish to target, you might have to consider different copy for each advertisement. An extreme example of this would be if you decided to advertise for a heating and ventilation engineer in a trade magazine to target engineers already working in the industry, and in the black press to encourage applications from the black community. To address the different concerns or interests of both groups, it's most likely that you would probably use different copy in the advertisements.

It is impossible to supply you with an example of a perfect advertisement, because every advertisement needs to be tailored to its audience and that makes every advertisement different. However, almost all good advertisements include the following ingredients:

113

- **noticeability** – your advertisement must be noticed by your target audience. Graphics, unusual designs, or prominent words/job titles are quite good ways of raising the profile of an advertisement. The use of boxes, bold type or several columns help the message stand out but will, of course, increase the cost. Always include your organisation's name as 'blind' advertisements breed suspicion rather than interest.

- **accurate message** – your advertisement will almost certainly contain a description of the job, what it is like to work in the organisation, and an indication of the benefits. These should be accurate, concise, engaging, and written in a natural and easily understood manner. You should ask yourself, and answer in the advertisement, the question 'what is it that applicants want to know?'

- **method of application** – you must tell people how to pursue their interest in the position. Do you want them to write or phone for an application form and further details? Can they send a CV? To whom should they write? Some organisations use answer phones to record requests for application forms. When a certain number of calls have been received, the answer phone becomes 'engaged' to limit the number of applications received. This is a rather unprofessional way to treat people, and it may exclude many suitable candidates. Such a procedure simply highlights a failure to analyse, understand, and target appropriate segments properly.

■ **non-discriminatory** – you must avoid referring to gender, race or marital status in advertisements for legal reasons unless there is a genuine occupational requirement (see chapter 2). Be careful of hidden discriminatory language such as words like 'he' to refer to the job, or 'salesman' or 'barmaid' which have an in built gender suggestion. Sales person or bar staff, possibly followed by (male/female) is much better and avoids the problem.

Many organisations add phrases such as 'We would welcome applications from people with disabilities' in an effort to encourage such people to apply. Does this work? Unfortunately, there has been no research into people's reactions to these comments. A cynic might say that these statements reveal an organisation with an unbalanced labour force who wants to give the impression of attending to the problem. These statements are worth considering, but the problem seems to arise because several segments are being targeted at once. Would two advertisements in different and better targeted media be more appropriate?

114

Can you write an advertisement for the vacancy in the warehouse?

Choose one of the market segments we identified for the post of shift manager in a clothing distribution warehouse:

■ current employees in supervisory or managerial positions
■ managers in similar positions in other distribution warehouses
■ management consultants and temporary staff who specialise in solving distribution management problems
■ members of racial groups that are under-represented in the organisation who have the relevant diplomacy and problem solving skills
■ project managers in direct contact with customers
■ production controllers in direct contact with customers.

Which market segment are you going to target?

What newspaper, journal, magazine or other medium do you think will be most successful in reaching the attention of the target audience? Why?

Choose one of the media you identified. Write a draft advertisement to attract applicants from this segment.

Did you include all the ingredients mentioned above?

- *Will it be noticed by your target market?*
- *Does it contain a realistic and accurate message?*
- *Does it tell readers how to apply?*
- *Have you avoided using discriminatory language?*

An advertisement targeted at managers in similar positions in other distribution warehouses might be best placed in a suitable trade magazine. It could look like the one shown below.

RETAIL TRADE DISTRIBUTION

Distribution Warehouse Shift Manager

Wednesbury Warehouse   18–24K + Bonus

Retail Trade Distribution is an independent company serving major retailers across Great Britain. Your role will be to manage five 8-hour shifts per week of the clothing distribution line within budget. You will be responsible for the full and complete dispatch of orders according to the customer's requirements. The ideal candidate must be able to demonstrate:

- the ability to solve and prevent people related problems arising
- the ability to manage commercial relationships with external customers
- the ability to work within a highly regulated environment.

In addition, the ideal candidate should be able to demonstrate abilities in:

- planning and co-ordination
- training.

Finally, the ideal candidate will have a thorough understanding of managing people in a distribution warehouse.

For further information and an application form, please phone Chris Gormley on (0121) 987 6543 or fax us on (0121) 987 6666. Alternatively, you can request further details by EMail.
Our EMail address is: gormley@retailtrade.co.uk.

Please quote reference number RTD224 on all correspondence.

WE ARE AN EQUAL OPPORTUNITIES EMPLOYER

115

The sample contains all of the ingredients of a good advertisement. But is it sufficiently eye-catching to attract a suitable response? Unfortunately only trial and error will tell you this.

Stage 4: Evaluate the response   The final stage of advertisement design is to measure the effectiveness of the adverts you use. For future reference, you need to know how effective different designs and media are, and whether you were successful in getting the required response from your target markets. The only way to do this is to monitor the performance of each piece of recruitment material. A useful trick is to give each advertisement a separate reference number so that you can track respondents. It is useful to keep figures on:

- the cost of each advertisement
- the total number of people requesting an application form
- the number returning the application form
- the number shortlisted and offered employment from each advertisement.

From this information, you can calculate the cost of attracting each applicant by market segment, the cost of each shortlisted applicant by market segment, the value of each advertisement, and so on.

116

Recruiting through third parties
■ ■ ■

There is, of course, an alternative to attracting applicants yourself: you can pay someone to do it for you. There are two main types of third party that you can use. They adopt the rather grand titles of:

- executive selection consultants
- executive search consultants.

You probably know executive search consultants by another name: headhunters. Although using consultants can be expensive with no guarantee of success, it is worth considering both methods. Once you take the hidden costs into account, both search and selection consultants can be good value and might find excellent people for you that you couldn't find yourself.

How much are you prepared to spend on finding new members of staff? How much do you value your staff? In 1988, Mazda spent about $13,000 per employee to staff the assembly line in its new car plant in Flat Rock, Michigan. This is as much as they invest in recruiting senior managers through executive search (headhunters). They regard it as money well spent.

Executive selection consultants

Executive selection consultants are people who will attract staff for you by placing advertisements. If you look at the job advertisements in the national press you'll see that about half of the display advertisements are placed by third parties on behalf of client organisations. As you can just as easily place your own advertisements, why are they used? There are several advantages:

- because they place advertisements regularly, these consultants can buy space at much cheaper rates than you can (and they might have advance block bookings on the 'best space')
- they have expertise in designing advertisements
- they can help you with organisational entry analysis and the preparation of selection criteria
- they will take the administration of the process off your hands
- they can narrow down the applicants to a shortlist of the most suitable respondents
- they are best suited to situations when you need to attract people with specific skills and experience that can't be found through agencies
- advertisements might be seen by suitable people not looking for work who might respond because they are curious – they have greater coverage than agencies which only carry people actively looking for work.

117

Unfortunately, the quality of executive selection consultants varies greatly. Some will carry out all the above. Others will simply place an advertisement for you and then dump a pile of CVs on your desk, which somewhat reduces the benefit of using them. This is particularly relevant when you consider that a poorly targeted advertisement in the national press can easily attract several thousand replies (25,000 is neither unknown nor uncommon). This problem can be easily avoided by specifying at an early stage of the relationship with the consultant exactly what duties you expect them to perform.

There are several disadvantages to using executive selection consultants:

- advertising may not be the best way of reaching your target audience
- suitable people simply might not see your advertisement
- there are relatively few vacancies which require large scale advertisements that poorly address market segments

- it can become very costly (a typical fee would be 15-20% of starting salary plus the cost of advertising space which can make them as expensive, if not more expensive, than headhunters)

- there are no guarantees of success – what do you do if no one responds to the advertisement?

- how do you control the quality of the work carried out on your behalf?

Does your organisation use an executive selection consultant to advertise its vacancies?

- If it does, what constraints does this place on you?
- If it does not, is there a policy stopping you from using them?

Executive search consultants (headhunters)

118

Headhunters like to keep their activities shrouded in mystery. By doing so, they hope to produce an aura of 'people of power' who shape the boardrooms of organisations. They want to be respected, but fear they're viewed as pimps or slave traders who deal in people for money. The protectionist aura that surrounds headhunters doesn't really help them because as many people are scared off by the image as impressed by it. This is unfortunate because headhunting is, in many ways, the perfect form of recruitment that can be used to attract the most suitable applicants to a wide variety of vacancies.

What do headhunters do? How do they operate? As there is some mystique regarding how they go about their work, I shall explain the headhunting process. Headhunters:

- develop an understanding of the vacancy and the organisation
- analyse the industry and the major players in it to produce an initial list of contacts
- phone these initial contacts and ask them 'who would you recommend in this field?' or 'who do you think can help me find a suitable person?'
- the people identified as the best candidates are approached and interviewed
- once the consultant is sure that a suitable shortlist has been produced, they draw up a report and present it with the shortlist to the client
- the people on the shortlist are invited to meet the client

- when the client makes their choice, the consultant acts as an independent go-between to negotiate terms and conditions.

Headhunters are used in the following circumstances:

- when there are very few people who could do the job
- when very few people would apply for the job
- when the people you want to apply are not looking for a job
- when people need to be persuaded to apply for the job
- when the egos of applicants need to be massaged
- when the potential applicants are spread very thinly
- when a highly specific combination of skills is required
- when you want to recruit an intact team
- when you want to find out who the major players in the field are
- when you want to protect your own staff from a headhunter (many headhunters guarantee not to poach your staff for a couple of years after the last assignment you give them terminates)
- when the potential applicants can be researched – this is usually only possible when suitable applicants have contact with people in other organisations (sales vacancies can be researched by asking purchasing staff their impressions of salespeople and vice versa).

119

There are a number of problems associated with using headhunters:

- they need time to do their work – usually it takes at least a month for a shortlist to emerge
- they are associated with senior appointments and may not be willing to take on lower level vacancies
- it is critical that the headhunter forms an excellent understanding of the job and the organisation
- some delegate the research work – probably the most important aspect of any search – to less able assistants
- many headhunts are unsuccessful
- they can be expensive – between 25 and 33% of starting package is normal – but increasingly headhunters will carry out work for a set fee, possibly as low as £4500, and limit expenses to 10% of the total fee
- consultant expenses can dramatically inflate the cost
- some headhunters turn a search into a trawl of their existing databases which limits them to the strengths and weaknesses of agencies (but at headhunter charge rates)
- many headhunters have an expertise in a particular industry or

type of recruitment and they might not be prepared to accept work away from their specialism

- headhunters may not carry out work for you if it conflicts with the interests of their current clients

- using an industry expert might bar you from taking staff from a competitor for whom the consultant also works

- many people find it flattering to be approached by a headhunter and can waste your time by pursuing their interest without ever intending to accept the job

- they can be quite persuasive and can convince people to accept jobs when it isn't in their best interests which, in the longer term, is rarely in your best interests

- headhunters change the balance of power in the relationship between organisation and employee – as the applicant has been approached on the strength of their reputation they can respond with, 'I'm very happy where I am thank you; make it worth my while'.

120

In summary, headhunting is a highly targeted form of recruitment which can be the solution to particularly difficult vacancies. That said, headhunters are increasingly taking on a wider range of vacancies, that could be filled by other methods, for a set fee that is comparable with agencies. Don't rule out headhunters because you think they might be too expensive. They can be used most cost effectively for a wide range of jobs.

Managing consultants

Experiences with consultants differ widely. Some managers swear by their consultants and would never use any other recruitment method to attract staff. Other managers swear at their consultants and would never use them again. There are a few simple things you can do to ensure that you don't fall into this second category.

The first rule of working with consultants is to pick them very carefully. Headhunt your consultant. There are many people you could ask about whom to use. Headhunters just pick up the phone and call people. Why don't you? A few calls to personnel or human resource managers in your industry are a good way to start. Most people are happy to help and give you advice. In particular, ask about:

- fees and expenses
- how long assignments have taken
- success rates
- the type of vacancies they have been used for

- the quality of the people attracted
- the strengths and weaknesses of the consultant.

Once you've decided which consultants to approach, there are several ways to proceed. The easiest is to invite the consultant in and talk through their way of handling an assignment. An alternative method is to hold a 'beauty parade' where you ask several consultants to compete against each other for the work. Beauty parades take time to organise and there's no evidence to suggest that you get a better consultant. Some anecdotal evidence suggests the opposite and that beauty parades cause problems, because some consultancies will put their 'star performers' on show and, if they win, delegate the assignment to less able colleagues.

Once you've chosen your consultant, you want them to develop a thorough understanding of your organisation and, in particular, your organisation's culture. Most headhunters are able to ascertain whether people can do the job through peer evaluations and recommendations (most of the people headhunters put forward will already be doing a similar job effectively). The best headhunters have the skill to be able to assess how well the person will transfer to your organisation. Will it be an environment in which they can thrive? To be able to do this, they must thoroughly understand your organisation's culture, which means they have to get close to you. You need to form a relationship with the consultant where there is mutual trust. Given the closeness of the relationship you want to foster, you need certain assurances that your trust will not be breached. This is a powerful reason why you need a contract to manage the relationship with a consultant.

121

Contracts with headhunters

There are several items that you need to spell out in your contract.

- How will the fee be calculated? Is it based on a percentage of base salary, or will commissions, bonuses, and incentives be included? Or will it be a set fee?

- How will the fee be paid? Will it be paid in tranches? What events will trigger the payments? (A normal fee structure is one third up front, one third on the production of a satisfactory shortlist and assignment report, one third when the new recruit starts.)

- Who will do the research?

- Who will conduct interviews with applicants?

- Over what time scale will the assignment be conducted? What happens if a shortlist isn't forthcoming in the required time scale?

- What guarantees do you require?
- What happens if the headhunter fails to find you a suitable person?
- What happens if the new recruit leaves within six months of joining the organisation? (Some headhunters will conduct a new headhunt either free – except for expenses – or at a much lower rate.)
- What reports do you require during the assignment? (A weekly phone call and a written report every two or three weeks should be the minimum you expect. You want to be sure that the consultant is getting on with your assignment.)
- What should the reports contain? Do you also want a survey of the main players and salary rates in the industry? Are you willing to pay extra for this?
- What guarantees do you require preventing the headhunter poaching your own staff for other clients?
- What can sources and potential candidates be told about the job and the organisation? (Many organisations insist that the name of the recruiting organisation is kept secret until the client agrees to interview the applicant.)
- For your own protection, there should be a confidentiality clause in the contract.

A cautionary note

Don't be forced to use the first consultant you come across, or to use any consultant simply because they've been highly recommended by someone. The executive selection and search industries are very competitive. If you aren't happy with what the consultant tells you, or how they plan to conduct the assignment, kick 'em out. There are plenty more around that would die for your business.

> If headhunters won't give you what you want, kick 'em out.

Are internal applicants different?
■ ■ ■

In these days of political correctness, internal candidates are treated identically to external candidates. They have to fill in application forms and are informed of selection decisions in the same way as external candidates (by brief impersonal letter). Anything internal candidates want taken into consideration must be introduced by them during the selection process, and selection panels ignore anything that hasn't emerged during interviews or selection tests.

This is madness. One of the key tasks of selectors is to find out as much relevant information about applicants as possible so that the best decision might be made. To exclude reliable information so as to treat everyone identically simply reduces everything to the lowest common denominator. You will always know more about some people than others. With internal candidates, you have much more information already to hand. Why not use it? If you know more about some people than others, then that's to everyone's advantage.

Problems arise in two ways. The first problem occurs when it isn't just the extra information that is used to assess internal candidates. Selectors can easily get distracted when assessing internal candidates and their evaluation can become contaminated by their friendship with the candidate, or simply the inconvenience of having to compare internal with external candidates. In many cases, in the short term it seems much easier to select an internal candidate. It also avoids the terrible problem of having to tell a friend or colleague that they've been unsuccessful.

123

The second type of problem concerns the halo and horns effect. The extra information you have about internal candidates makes up your mind before you interview them. If your feelings are generally negative, they have no chance. If your feelings are positive, then they're in the running. But, as we all know, the unknown and undiscovered are strangely attractive. So a good external candidate has the aura of forbidden fruit, and this aura can make the capable internal candidate seem mundane in comparison.

There are no simple answers to these problems except to reiterate the importance of comparing all applicants to the selection criteria. In the next chapter, I'll illustrate another aspect of this problem; that the profiles of internal and external candidates are very different and call upon the selector to make different types of decisions.

Are internal candidates different?

How would you respond if your current organisation replied to your internal application with the following letter?

Dear Ms Page,

Thank you for your application.

I must inform you that on this occasion your application has been unsuccessful.

Thank you for your interest in our organisation.

Yours sincerely,

pp Mary Moron

Richard Head
Director of Human Resource Assets

124

> *Unfortunately, this type of letter is far too common. In an effort to treat every applicant equally, the correspondence becomes bland and indifferent. Have you been in this situation where you've been rejected for an internal promotion? How did being rejected feel? How did you react? Internal candidates are different because they will come to work tomorrow. The manner in which they are treated will have an effect on their motivation and satisfaction. Employees usually only apply for jobs that they think they are genuinely suited to. They know the risks of failure – it can be embarrassing, a hurdle to future promotion, and very dispiriting. Consequently, internal candidates do warrant special treatment. These are current employees, they will go to work tomorrow with their psychological contracts changed, they need to be treated differently and with sensitivity.*

Choosing recruitment techniques

Earlier in this chapter, you looked at the market segments you could target for your vacancies and at suitable media. Now that you've looked at other methods of recruitment, are any methods more appropriate than advertisements? Why?

SUMMARY – CHAPTER 6 *ATTRACTION*

- The purpose of recruitment is to attract a small number of highly suitable applicants.

- The golden rule of recruitment: 'tell it like it is'.

- Realistic job previews can be used to:
  – reduce inflated expectations
  – inflate depressed expectations.

- Corporate advertising in job advertisements can confound your message and increase response rates without increasing quality.

- You should target the market segments you wish to penetrate:
  – identify the segments
  – understand the segments
  – decide which segments to target.

- Recruitment market segments should be:
  – measurable
  – substantial
  – accessible
  – actionable.

- Internal candidates need to be treated reasonably and with special attention.

- Job advertisements should be:
  – noticeable
  – accurate
  – informative about the method of application
  – non-discriminatory.

- Executive selection consultants can take much of the hassle of recruitment off your hands.

- Headhunters are a highly targeted form of recruitment that can work out to be quite cost effective.

- If consultants won't give you what you want, kick 'em out.

7

■ ■ ■

How do you assess applicants?

CHAPTER OBJECTIVES

After reading this chapter you should be able to:
- select the applicants which best satisfy the selection criteria from application forms and CVs
- choose appropriate selection techniques
- organise an interview
- develop interview questions that gather evidence against the selection criteria
- write a letter requesting a reference
- select the best candidate.

CHAPTER OVERVIEW

Assessing applicants should be one of the easiest and most straight-forward parts of the whole organisational entry process. If you have conducted your organisational entry analysis effectively, then the assessment phase is simply a matter of comparing each of the applicants to the selection criteria and choosing the best. The two most common forms of selection – shortlisting and interviewing – and the alternative methods that you can use to assess applicants are examined in this chapter. I look at the strengths and weaknesses of references, and end by looking at the rejection of applicants.

Shortlisting

■ ■ ■

Shortlisting is the initial filtering of applications to decide which you wish to pursue. It needs to be carried out systematically. You should rely on the essential and desirable selection criteria to determine which people to accept and which to reject; if possible, only people who satisfy all the essential criteria should be shortlisted. No one should be shortlisted if you have evidence that they cannot satisfy any of the essential criteria.

Shortlisting becomes difficult when your recruitment has gone wrong and you have too many or too few applicants. When you have too many applicants, the problem is one of reduction. With hundreds of application forms or CVs to read, it can be tremendously difficult to be thorough and give every candidate an even chance. The selection ratio in this stage (the number chosen divided by the total number considered) is at its lowest, and it is very easy to leave excellent candidates in the pile. To prevent this happening you need to remain systematic and apply your essential criteria rigorously. A recruitment manager of a large multinational company related the following example to me.

'We had thousands of applicants for our graduate entry programme. We had so many that we had to recruit temporary staff to process the mountain of application forms! Shortlisting was a nightmare. We started by rejecting everyone who didn't have a 2.2. After ten minutes, we revised our criteria and insisted on 2.1s. But even that was hopeless. In the end, we only gave first interviews to graduates with firsts from 'quality' universities and people with relevant master's degrees.'

Shortlisting is also problematic when you haven't got enough, or any, suitable applicants. If you experience this problem, you need to examine your recruitment procedures to see whether it was simply poor marketing of the position that caused the problem (in which case you would probably choose to repeat the recruitment stage), or whether no one with the required skills wants to apply for the vacancy. If this is the case, you need to return to your organisational entry analysis and examine whether your selection criteria are realistic. If they are not, you should revise them and see whether suitable applicants have applied. Otherwise you will need to advertise the job again. On no account should you shortlist people you know cannot satisfy your essential selection criteria. It is a waste of your time and a waste of their time.

Who would you shortlist?

The following details have been taken from CVs submitted by candidates for the post of Distribution Warehouse Shift Manager. The job description and the selection criteria can be found in Chapter 5. Imagine that you have already shortlisted three good candidates who satisfy all the essential criteria, and you want to shortlist one more person. Who would you choose and why?

	Albert Mullin	*Silke Hauptmann*	*Andrew Baker*
Address	Suburbs	Town 50 miles away	City centre
Date of birth	01/05/1938	23/04/1970	14/09/1967
Nationality	British	German	British
Current employer	Rubber Goods plc	Retail Trade Distribution	Unemployed
Size of employer	£80m turnover p.a.	£35m turnover p.a.	N/A
Position held	Distribution Manager	Shift supervisor	N/A
Staff managed	Thirty	Eight	N/A
No. of previous employers	One	Two	One
Qualifications	Institute of Purchasing and Supply	None	None
Level of computing skill	Expert with spreadsheets and databases	Basic WP and spreadsheets	Good spreadsheets, wp and EMail
Distribution management skills	Strong	Adequate	Good
Clothing distribution experience	None	Yes	None
Management experience	35 years: up to senior level	3 years: junior positions	6 years: up to middle mgt

Customer contact	Continual	None	Regular in previous job
Suitable values	No evidence	Yes	No evidence
Knowledge of the operation	Similar type of work	Yes	Similar type of work
Training skills	No evidence	None	Previous experience as a trainer
Planning and co-ordination skills	Strong at senior mgt level	No experience	Yes
Report writing	Yes	No experience	Yes
Health and Safety certification	No	Yes	Yes
Numeracy	Strong	'A' level equivalent	'O' level maths
Education	No school certificate	Abitur	6 'O' levels
Further education	Certificate in Management	Diploma in Management	MBA
Court convictions	None	None	Driving offence
Disabilities	None	None	Wheelchair user
Other information		Fluent English, German and French	
Reason for applying	None given	Advancement	Needs a suitable job

129

- Who would you shortlist?

- Why did you make this choice?

This exercise illustrates how difficult shortlisting can be. On the face of it, a case could be made for any of the three candidates. Applicants were asked to send a copy of their CV, and as a result you haven't got all the information you would like to make your choice. Had a specific application form been used, it could have asked questions which gathered information on the selection criteria. Some of the information displayed in the table had to be extracted from short pieces of narrative. As a result, at this stage you have to assume that experience gained on a criterion is good experience. Obviously, when you test or interview the person, you would gather evidence to check these assumptions.

How do you make a choice? Perhaps the best way is to rearrange the data, drawing attention to the selection criteria.

Essential criteria	Albert Mullin	Silke Hauptmann	Andrew Baker
Prevention of people related problems	Yes	Yes	Yes
Customer care	Yes	None	Yes
Suitable values	Can't say	Yes	Can't say

Desirable criteria	Albert Mullin	Silke Hauptmann	Andrew Baker
Planning	Yes	None	Yes
Training	Can't say	None	Yes
Common sense	Can't say	Yes	Can't say
Knowledge of the operation	Partial	Yes	Partial

Supplementary criteria	Albert Mullin	Silke Hauptmann	Andrew Baker
Report writing	Yes	None	Yes
Health and Safety	No	Yes	Yes

Analysing each of the candidates by comparing their qualities to the selection criteria helps to identify whom to shortlist and whom to reject. The golden rule with shortlisting is that failure to meet an essential criterion is a reason to reject someone. Silke Hauptmann has not had the experience of managing customer relationships. But, being an internal candidate, the person doing the shortlisting should seek the opinion of her line manager about her ability to do this. This extra information is important and should be taken into account. For the purpose of this exercise though, we'll assume that this extra information suggests that she would fail to meet the criterion. Therefore, we must reject her.

The profiles of Albert Mullin and Andrew Baker are remarkably similar. For both, you cannot determine one of the essential criteria (the interpersonal skills and suitable values) but this doesn't represent a critical failure as the issue is that you don't have information on the criterion, not that they haven't got the required ability. You know that Andrew Baker possesses one of the desirable criteria (training) that you want, which Albert Mullin does not. In addition, Andrew Baker has certification in Health and Safety which Albert Mullin does not. Andrew Baker, therefore, seems the person to shortlist. There are two final checks to make:

131

- do any of the candidates who satisfy the essential criteria so excel at any of the desirable criteria that this should be given extra weight?
- am I shortlisting the best of a bad lot? Should I shortlist no one? Remember that inviting someone in who is clearly going to be unsuitable is a waste of everyone's time.

This method of shortlisting is recommended for several reasons:

- you concentrate on the vital knowledge, skills, abilities and other characteristics (KSAOs) that you know are vital for performance in the job
- you eliminate non-job related distractions (such as Andrew Baker's wheelchair and Albert Mullin's age, both of which are irrelevant to this job)
- you are systematic
- you make a rational decision
- you can justify to an independent third party why you have chosen the people on your shortlist
- all applicants are treated fairly.

Internal versus external candidates

This exercise also illustrates how the profiles of internal candidates differ to those of external candidates. The internal candidate typically applies from a junior position. They might exhibit promise in their current job, and you are able to assess how well they fit in, their motivation and job satisfaction. You have to make the decision whether they are ready to 'move up'. The external candidate tends to be someone who has the experience and proven skills in a similar or related job. The decision here is whether you think the person will transfer their skills and abilities to your organisation. Could they 'move across'? With internal candidates the risk is that they won't develop their skills. With external candidates the risk is that they won't fit in and won't transfer their skills.

Lessons for shortlisting

This exercise demonstrates some important lessons for shortlisting:

- produce a grid of the selection criteria and list the relevant information on every applicant against each one

- eliminate any one who fails to meet any of the essential criteria

- you should proactively seek out extra information relevant to the selection criteria on internal candidates where possible

- only factors in the selection criteria should be taken into account

- always check at the end that you're not being forced into shortlisting the best of an unsuitable bunch of applicants.

Selection methods

■ ■ ■

The purpose of selection

Although shortlisting is normally associated with the initial phases of selection, it demonstrates very clearly the principle underlying all selection: you want to gather as much relevant information as possible and then compare applicants to the selection criteria ignoring all other factors. There are traditional selection techniques you can use (interviews, intelligence tests, personality tests, assessment centres and so on), but there is no reason why you shouldn't create your own selection tests if they give you high quality information on the selection criteria. For example, we've been looking at the job of a shift manager in a distribution warehouse. One of the essential selection criteria we identified was the ability to manage relationships with external customers. You might automatically think that interviews are the way to assess this, but there are alternatives. You could construct role plays or simulations that investigate how each applicant responds to particular customer related problems.

The choice of selection technique is yours. You need to pick techniques that:

■ test applicants against the selection criteria

■ give results you know how to use

■ do not discriminate against genders, races, or married people

■ will be viewed by applicants as appropriate and relevant to the job.

The variety of selection techniques

Although nothing should stop you developing your own selection techniques if they will give you the information you need to make the best possible decision, I should note that several types of test dominate selection. Interviews are used by virtually every organisation for every vacancy. Personality, literacy, numeracy and intelligence tests are now used by about half the organisations in Britain for some of their vacancies. The frequency of use of selection tests can be portrayed graphically (see Fig 7.1).

133

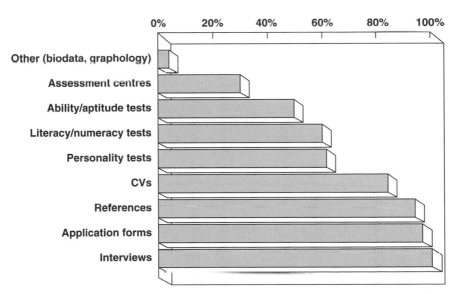

Fig 7.1 Frequency of use of selection techniques by organisations in the UK

At this point in other books on recruitment and selection, there is commonly a second graph or table which shows the comparative effectiveness of each of the techniques. In a book for a practitioner audience, this sort of list can distort the most important message when choosing selection techniques. You want to choose the most appropriate and useful techniques for testing people against the selection criteria. Sometimes this will be the techniques which have been shown to be best at predicting future performance over a range of jobs, and sometimes it will be the less highly rated techniques. For example, references have been shown to be one of the worst selection methods, but, as I'll demonstrate at the end of the chapter, they are an important part of most organisational entry processes. For this reason, when I look at selection techniques, I prefer to focus on their strengths and weaknesses and the situations in which they are most appropriate.

Selection tests or screening tests?

Why does everyone use an interview to select people? How are they used? It seems that interviews are used to draw the threads together, and to determine whether or not to offer the job to someone. The interview is a selection device. But what of the other selection tests? Are they used to determine whom to employ? Sometimes, yes. But more often, the other forms of selection test (e.g. literacy and numeracy tests) are used to produce evidence on specific criteria to inform the interviewer. As such, these tests might more properly be termed screening tests; it is unusual for definite decisions to be based on them. It is much more likely that they'll be used to weed out unsuitable candidates or produce specific information. This suggests that organisational entry processes often combine selection and screening techniques to enable selectors to make the best possible decision.

Psychometric tests

The term 'psychometric test' covers a number of different types of cognitive or psychological tests.

Intelligence tests

A strong argument can be made for the use of intelligence tests. In many jobs, high intelligence is strongly associated with high performance. Also, higher intelligence should help a newcomer:

- adapt to the new environment quickly and smoothly
- pick up a job quickly
- find solutions to unpredictable and unusual problems.

In addition, intelligence has been shown to be quite consistent across different environments.

Important though these justifications are, they don't mean that intelligence tests should be adopted in every situation. People generally don't like completing them and, if they don't deem them appropriate for the position, they might opt out of the process. It might be argued that the tests discover who's good at doing tests, rather than who's highly intelligent. Another important factor is that intelligence tests can prompt you into decisions that ignore many other key points. Intelligence tests tend to concentrate on a particular type of intelligence (spatial, problem solving, inductive, deductive, reasoning, and so on) and ignore everything else. Jobs that require a high degree of intelligence also tend to need common sense, practical intelligence, experience of similar situations, communication skills, specific knowledge, political skills, interpersonal skills and so on. As a result, an intelligence test is likely to be only one component in an organisational entry process.

135

Personality tests

Personality tests have been popular for selection throughout the twentieth century. The use of personality tests stems from the belief that you can measure personalities and they predict how people will perform at work. Unfortunately, although there are all manner of personality tests around, no one has yet shown that they predict people's work behaviour accurately and reliably. They may give indications about people's behaviour, but not definitive statements. At best, they arc only a moderate predictor of how well someone will perform at work. Personality tests have these problems for several reasons:

■ they isolate internal factors and ignore how people interact with environmental factors, which have been shown to play a significant role in determining human behaviour

■ they commonly measure personality on a small number of factors, which prompt the recruiter into generalisations

■ how do you know what type of personality traits a job requires?

As a result, personality tests tend to be used in one of two ways:

■ as a screening device to spot those people who would clearly be unsuitable for the job

■ as a career choice device for school leavers or graduates to see which typo of caroor might be best suited to them

What personality traits do you need?

Think about your own job. From the following list of personality traits, indicate the personality profile of the ideal person in your current job.

Stable ————————————	Unstable
Confident ————————————	Hesitant
Talkative ————————————	Shy
Introverted ————————————	Extroverted
Practical ————————————	Imaginative
Trusting ————————————	Suspicious
Competitive ————————————	Teamworker
Tolerant ————————————	Critical
Conservative ————————————	Radical
Friendly ————————————	Aloof
Objective ————————————	Subjective
Cold ————————————	Emotional
Masculine ————————————	Feminine

136

These personality traits were picked at random from a number of questionnaires. They do not form a selection device and must not be used as one. The purpose of this exercise is to highlight some of the problems with personality tests:

- *how do you determine what constitutes the ideal personality for a job?*
- *the categories are evenly spread and may give added emphasis to an unimportant trait*
- *the variables are not always exact antonyms which causes rating problems*
- *the variables often have descriptive names to encapsulate a number of other factors, the complexity of which might be lost in the results (what do the terms masculine and feminine mean, for example? do they discriminate unfairly?)*
- *the results and some of the terminology require interpretation which might lead to false conclusions*
- *the very fact that you concentrate on finding the 'correct' traits for your job and in filling in the questionnaire distracts you from other important factors related to the job*
- *these tests can divert your attention from the selection criteria*
- *they offer a 'pseudo-science' that can give the results of the tests a disproportionate influence in the selection decision.*

Literacy and numeracy tests

Fortunately the days when large numbers of children left school unable to read and write are behind us. Educational technology has advanced along with the skills of teachers. For employers, this means that most sixteen and eighteen year old people they meet have reasonable levels of reading, writing and arithmetic. However, as some will be better than others, this difference in ability is a useful way to differentiate between applicants. Literacy and numeracy tests are also useful for unskilled or semiskilled posts where the incumbent needs a particular level of the '3Rs'. In situations where reading, writing or numerical ability is an important selection criterion, these tests are a valuable screening device that you would be wise to consider using.

Obtaining and using psychometric tests

Many people are put off using these tests because they don't know how to get hold of them, or how to administer them. This is unfortunate because, as I've said, there are many circumstances when they can play an important role in an organisational entry process.

Some of the simpler tests, such as reading and writing tests, can be obtained quite easily or designed yourself. The best place to start looking for them is the trade press. Alternatively, you might call either the Institute of Personnel and Development or the British Psychological Society for advice. You'll find their addresses and phone numbers at the back of the book.

For more complex or sophisticated intelligence or personality tests, there are two considerations. First, you will probably have to go through chartered psychologists to get access to the better tests. Secondly, the person administering the tests needs to have certain certification. If you work in a large organisation, you'll almost certainly find it has people with the required skills. If you don't, then you can hire qualified people to do the testing for you. Alternatively, you could get qualified yourself. You would need to take a couple of week long courses run by one of four or five chartered psychologists. These courses are not cheap, and it will cost you between £2000 and £3000 to get the qualification. It will also take time. For more information on how to do this, contact the British Psychological Society.

One ethical principle relating to testing is worth stressing. If you submit applicants to psychometric tests, you should offer them feedback on the findings.

Analogous tests

Analogous tests are also known as work samples; they ask the candidate to undertake the job they've applied for, or a realistic simulation. These tests have the massive benefit that you get to see how well the person does in the job and, sometimes, the environment as well. The ultimate form of selection would be to get the applicants to carry out the actual work for a prolonged period, but this is rarely possible (see temporary to regular recruitment in the previous chapter). So asking applicants to have a go at a realistic simulation or an abbreviated form of the job is highly advantageous. It is also likely that analogous tests correlate closely to the selection criteria.

Analogous tests have been developed, or can easily be developed by you, for several categories of jobs, including:

- typing and word processing
- accounting
- bricklaying
- computer maintenance.

My gym uses analogous tests to very good effect. It runs more than fifty aerobics classes a week and consequently has a constant demand for new aerobics instructors. How do they assess them? Well, as you might imagine, they ask potential instructors to run a class or two. Qualified instructors and a gym manager take the class as participants along with about thirty regular punters. The applicants are paid at the appropriate rate and interviewed by a manager who took the class. Meanwhile, opinion from the regulars is canvassed regarding how much they enjoyed the session and whether they would come back next week, which is how the instructor would be judged if taken on. All this information is combined to make the selection decision.

An alternative type of analogous test is the assessment of portfolios. Designers, academics and actors are all commonly judged on their past performance in similar roles. Portfolio assessment can be quite powerful as long as you remember to analyse how well performance in one environment will transfer to your environment.

Unfortunately, analogous tests aren't perfect, and there are some drawbacks you need to consider:

- they are only suitable for some jobs
- they often isolate one skill in a job and ignore other important factors (for example, a typing test tells you how well someone can type, but it doesn't tell you anything about whether they'll turn up for work, how they'll get on with others, or the wide range of other skills they need)

■ they favour people who have done the job before or who respond to training quickly which might be good in the short term, but might not equate to longer term performance.

Analogous tests are so useful that some people have sought to extend the techniques to other jobs, including managerial vacancies. In-tray exercises and situational interviews are good examples of these. During an in-tray exercise, the applicants are asked to respond to or deal with items in a simulated in-tray as if they were doing the job. A situational interview is one where the interviewee is presented with a series of hypothetical situations and asked how they would respond to each one. These answers are judged on a predetermined scale against model answers supplied by experts, such as previous job holders. One of the drawbacks is that applicant's answers might not match what they would do in practice.

What analogous tests could you use?

Look at the selection criteria for the position you wish to fill. List the skills that they contain. Decide how you will measure each skill. Could you develop an analogous test for any of the skills?

Assessment centres

It is unfortunate that the term 'assessment centre' implies a place. In actual fact, this is a process where several tests are used in conjunction with each other. It just happens that when a number of tests are used in conjunction, it is usually best done at a special venue where applicants and assessors can escape the demands and interruptions of work. When you want to bombard the applicants with a large number of tests that take more than a day to administer, the assessment centre commonly becomes residential with an overnight stay.

An assessment centre might contain any of the tests mentioned already and usually includes interviews. But assessment centres are worth special mention because many of the tests typically employed in them can be separated out and used in a more normal organisational entry process to great advantage. You can develop these yourself or employ an occupational psychologist to help you. If your organisation has a personnel or human resources department, they're the best people to ask for help. The techniques that you might want to consider include:

■ **trial by sherry** – observation of how people behave in social situations

■ **presentations**

- **group work** – to assess interaction and behaviour in teams, monitor contribution levels, assess initiative and leadership qualities and so on
- **in-tray exercises**
- **simulations**
- **role plays**
- **case studies**
- **practical problem solving exercises.**

Assessment centres are sometimes called the 'Rolls Royce' method of selection because of the perceived high quality and thoroughness of the technique. As you might expect, with the costs of managers, psychologists, overnight stays, catering and so on, they also warrant the term because they are the most expensive of all selection techniques. The high cost of full-blown assessment centres means that they tend to be used by large organisations for the entry of future managers or for people who will hold positions of considerable responsibility, such as pilots or army officers.

Interestingly though, despite the cost and apparent thoroughness of assessment centres, they have been shown to be only moderately effective, and less effective than many of their component parts. There are a couple of reasons for this:

- they are artificial environments which might not reflect people's actual behaviour at work
- how do you combine results with contrasting indications?

The problem of combining results

The problems with assessment centres stem from their complexity and thoroughness. How do you combine the results of several tests each measuring something different? Imagine that you get the following results at an assessment centre for a graduate trainee.

	Alison Anderson	*Bronwen Bennett*	*Calum Cooper*
Role play	1st	2nd	3rd
Presentation	2nd	3rd	1st
In-tray	3rd	1st	2nd

Whom do you select? Why?

As you've probably guessed, this is a trick question. Firstly, it would be impossible to answer without seeing the selection criteria. Secondly, how do you go about comparing the results of different tests? The example in this reflective exercise illustrates a common problem: individuals are different and have different skills and abilities. Consequently, it can't be surprising that people perform differently in different types of test. The point of this exercise is to highlight one of the factors regarding the choice of selection techniques: you must know how you will use the results of your selection tests.

Interviews

■   ■   ■

Although methods other than interviews are increasingly used, numerous pieces of research have shown that interviews are the most commonly used of all selection methods. More than this, interviews are virtually universal, and it is likely that you will want to use them. The real benefit of interviews is that they are completely flexible and allow you to assess complex and interrelated issues.

Do you use interviews?

- Have you used interviews for selection?
- Did you make a conscious decision to use an interview?
- If you answered yes to the first question, why did you decide to use an interview?
- What are the strengths of the interview based on your experiences as an interviewer and an interviewee?
- From your experiences, what have you found to be the weaknesses of the interview?
- In what circumstances is an interview essential?
- In what circumstances would you not use an interview?

Almost all organisations in almost all circumstances use the interview at some stage in their selection process and it would be unusual if your organisation differed. Similarly, most applicants expect to be interviewed. Therefore, the suspicion is that many organisations don't actually make a rational decision to use an interview. When asked why an interview is used, the responses are likely to hint of post-event rationalism. Ask yourself how many of your responses could fall into this category.

Interviews are useful for assessing such personal characteristics as:

- interpersonal skills
- practical intelligence
- social interaction
- communication skills.

In addition to assessment, the interview can be used for:

- answering applicants' questions
- assessing complex issues
- selling the organisation
- negotiating terms and conditions.

It is a matter of some debate whether the interview accurately assesses ability at work, relevant experience and work skills. How often are a person's previous job title and responsibilities used to assess whether they have the skills to do the job? For example, 'she used to be a financial analyst at a major bank, therefore she is a good management accountant'. The key to good interviewing is the ability to ask the right questions: these probe for evidence related to the selection criteria.

There are circumstances when interviewing is almost the only technique that can be used. When recruiting through executive search consultants, for example, it is very difficult to insist that applicants should sit tests or supply evidence of competence. Their argument is likely to be 'as you approached me, you know I can do the job'.

Two final points need to be made about the interview:

- during the interview applicants form much of their impression of what it would be like to work in the unknown organisation. Therefore, the manner of the interview plays a major role in shaping the psychological contract between individual and organisation.
- the interview is the only technique which can be used to assess the interaction of individuals and environments. Many questions asked by interviewers probe into this interaction without realising it. By structuring a portion of the interview or adopting a semi-structured approach, you can gain evidence that should help you make objective interview decisions on organisational fit.

If you intend to use an interview there are several decisions that you must make:

- what is its purpose
- what venue to use and how it should be set up

- who needs to be involved in interviewing
- how the interview will be structured
- how the decision will be made.

The purpose of the interview

What are you trying to achieve with the interview? Do you want to assess the skills of the candidate? Do you want to 'sell' the organisation? Do you want the candidate to understand what it is really like to work in the organisation? Do you want the candidate to talk freely? Do you want to assess the type of environment that the candidate needs to perform well? Do you want to put the candidate under pressure? Your answers to questions such as these determine how you will construct the physical environment of the interview, who will be present, how it will be structured and how the decision will be made. You should design your interview in the way that best helps you achieve your purpose. However, that said, there are some guiding rules that should be adhered to by all interviewers.

143

The venue

First, you should ensure that you will not be interrupted. Disruptions break the concentration of both parties and make you appear most unprofessional. They give the impression that you care little about people.

The location sets the ambience. An office might appear formal, but it is often more relaxed as you tend to be more comfortable in your own office and it gives the candidate an opportunity to assess the working environment. A meeting room often appears more formal to the candidate. Desks act as barriers and can create a 'master and servant' atmosphere. It is more common these days for the parties to sit around a meeting table which can help with the exchange of information.

Two things are guaranteed to create a bad atmosphere in an interview. First, sit the interviewee so that they are looking into the sun and you are silhouetted against it. Second, give the interviewee a chair that is lower than yours. Both of these are very uncomfortable experiences.

Types of interview

Who needs to meet the candidate? Research has shown that most organisations interview candidates twice. This is also what applicants expect. The first interview tends to be a filtering interview to reveal which applicants match the selection criteria. The second interview is more geared to assessing the applicants' fit to the environment, to negotiate terms and conditions, and to answer the applicants' questions. If you decide to use two interviews and to split them in this way, then the first stage might be carried out by personnel staff and the second stage by yourself and other people who need to meet the candidate.

Who needs to be involved?

Who needs to be involved in the interviews for your vacancy? Why?

- You
- Your manager
- Your manager's manager
- Personnel staff
- External consultant
- Departmental staff
- Union representatives
- Independent third party
- Other

Once you have decided who needs to be involved, you must decide on the best way to involve them. Do they need to ensure that candidates are up to a certain standard? Do they need to be involved in the decision? Do they need to meet the successful candidate for approval? The role of the people in the process determines when they should be involved in the interviews.

One-to-one interviews

As the name suggests, these types of interview have two participants: the interviewer and the interviewee. These are the interviews preferred by interviewees and allow for the freest flow of information between the two parties. Although they have long been criticised by researchers as the least valid and least reliable form of selection, recent research has suggested fairly strongly that one-to-one interviews can be quite effective.

Panel interviews

In a panel interview, the applicant is interviewed by more than one interviewer at a time. It might simply involve two interviewers. But in some public services where many interest groups have to be represented, an interview panel of 20 people is not unknown.

What sort of interview would you prefer?

Would you prefer to be interviewed one-to-one or by a panel? Why?

> *The popularity of the one-to-one interview is probably because it is usually the most comfortable selection experience and the one in which the candidate feels they have the most control. The candidate feels less like a laboratory specimen and more like a human being. This has a significant impact on the effectiveness of the selection process. There is little point discovering the best candidate if, in doing so, the person is alienated to such an extent that a job offer is not accepted.*

Structure of interviews

Unstructured interviews

As you might imagine, an unstructured interview has no predetermined questions, or topics of conversation. Instead, interviewers are free to pursue any line of questioning they see fit. At the end of the interview, the interviewers assess the interviewees against the selection criteria based on what the interviewees have said. The unstructured interview is commonly criticised because it can lack rigour in an inexperienced person's hands and is open to a large number of problems. These include:

- impressions formed in the first five minutes greatly influence the selection decision and, therefore, can be based on very little information
- interviewers tend to look for reasons to reject rather than for reasons to accept interviewees which suggests that the 'least bad' applicant gets the job
- 'halo and horns' – the interviewer's perception of one good or one bad comment contaminates their perception of other comments
- appearance affects an interviewer's judgement
- it is difficult to assess skills and abilities in an interview.

Semi-structured interviews

In these the interviewer has a series of topics upon which to ask questions. This approach helps to keep the interview focused on the selection criteria, but does allow many of the above mentioned problems to enter the decision making.

145

Structured interviews

A structured interview is fully scripted and the interviewer asks every applicant the same questions. Interviewees' responses are rated on a predetermined scale. The advantage of this type of interview is that it eliminates most of the typical problems with interviews. But it puts the interviewer in a straitjacket and prevents them asking supplementary or follow up questions.

Episodic interviews

An episodic interview combines different types of structure. None of the above mentioned interviews is perfect and each type does different things well. The episodic interview is a response to this. Its greatest problem is the disruption of the atmosphere as it switches from structure to structure. In addition, interviewees might not fully acknowledge that the structure and purpose of the interview have changed.

Choosing a structure

Some interview structures seem to lend themselves naturally to certain objectives. For example, if you want to negotiate terms and conditions, or to sell the organisation, an unstructured format seems appropriate. On the other hand, if you are sure of the skills you are looking for, a structured approach is useful. The episodic approach acknowledges that there are different objectives and that each objective might be suited to a particular structure.

Making a decision

Perhaps the most difficult aspect of the entire organisational entry process is the framing of interview questions to produce evidence regarding the interviewee's suitability. Many questions asked by interviewers produce responses that tend to cause them to draw incorrect conclusions. For example, 'Peter's worked with spreadsheets in his job at Taylor Woodrow, therefore, he's got the spreadsheet skills that we want.'

Instead, the interviewer should say 'Peter says he's worked with spreadsheets at Taylor Woodrow, therefore we need to find out how good he is with spreadsheets'. There are two lessons here.

> ■ **You need to check your logic when assuming things during interviews.**
> ■ **Everything that someone says during an interview might be untrue.**

How do you counter this in an interview where you cannot, or do not want to, use other tests to examine the statements that people make? The answer lies in your framing of questions. Questions are either open or closed. An open question invites the respondent to speak and be expansive. A closed question, on the other hand, commonly elicits a 'yes' or 'no' answer. There are seven variants on open and closed questions.

- **Direct questions** – specific closed questions that require an exact answer. These are very good for clarifying or extracting information on key points. News presenters are particularly fond of them. An example would be 'tell me Minister, yes or no, are smaller class sizes better for children?' This example also demonstrates that such questions do not always receive the exact or accurate answer they expect.

- **Probing questions** – open questions designed to elicit additional detail. They often follow closed questions and frequently begin with the word 'why'. An example would be 'can you tell me why you decided to change to Apple computers from IBM-compatible computers?'

- **Leading questions** – these suggest or provoke a particular answer. They can be useful when you want to play devil's advocate and probe into how sycophantic the applicant is, but for the most part you want to avoid these questions as they rarely help you to understand the applicant better.

- **Loaded questions** – a form of leading question. The difference is that a loaded question uses emotive language. For example, 'do you really think black people are cut out to be managers?' These are almost always likely to be unfair and not related to the job. Avoid loaded questions at all costs.

- **Hypothetical questions** – these can be very useful when used to examine how people might react in particular situations. But if you overuse them, you might fail to address other important issues that simpler forms of questioning can examine.

- **Answering a question with a question** – skilled interviewers frequently shape their open questions in this way as they allow deeper probing into issues raised by interviewees without disrupting the natural flow. For example, 'Does the marketing department interfere with selling decisions?' 'Why do you ask?' They are also of benefit because they increase the percentage of time the interviewee talks. The danger is that overuse of this technique will make you sound evasive and shifty.

- **Mirror or reflective questions** – a form of open question where you turn a statement by the interviewee into a question;

i.e. you reflect it back at them. For example, 'So what you're saying is that you prefer to work alone?' Not only do these questions
ensure that you've understood the interviewee, but they also
allow you to probe deeper into the interviewee's statements.

AN INTERVIEW EXCHANGE

Pascale 'I'm interested in your computing skills. Could you tell
me something about your experience with computers?'

Juliet 'I was the financial analyst. This meant that I had to
produce all manner of information and reports on the
organisation's activities.'

Pascale 'What software did you use?'

Juliet 'A bit of a mixture; mainly Lotus 123 for Windows, but
also I would use AmiPro and occasionally I had to bring
things down from the mainframe.'

Pascale 'What information did you provide?'

Juliet 'A weekly sales report. That would compare the week
with the previous week and against budget and forecast. Also, I produced the departmental expenses that
goes to all budget holders. I also did project costings.
And there's a whole load of other stuff as well.'

Pascale 'How did you do the project costings?'

Juliet 'I'd liaise with the account manager and try to get an
estimate of the expected costs and the exact nature of
the project. I'd talk to other people that might be
involved such as the personnel manager to get a feel for
the hidden 'people' costs. This would all be fed into the
spreadsheet and that would tell us how profitable the
project would be.'

This is a typical interview exchange that uses both open and closed
questions. The following exercise examines the effectiveness of the
interviewer's questions. By analysing this exchange, I hope you'll
begin to separate good questions from bad. What information did Pascale gather?

Analysing an interview

Read the previous extract taken from an interview. What facts do you now
know about Juliet's computer skills?

Try to construct four alternative questions that would have gained better
quality evidence regarding Juliet's computer ability.

What does the exchange tell us about Juliet's computer skills? What facts do we know? Juliet claims to have been a financial analyst. She also claims to have produced reports and information about the organisation's activities. Juliet knows that Lotus 123 for Windows and AmiPro are software packages. Other than that, we are struggling to draw any firm conclusions. Yet this sort of exchange is typical. If it occurred during a one hour interview, the interviewer will only form a vague impression of the interviewee's skills, and the 'halo and horns' effect is likely to swing into operation. This exchange would make it possible for the interviewer to draw any conclusion they wanted about Juliet's computer abilities.

It is not always easy developing questions which produce evidence related to the selection criteria. You might have wanted to refer back to the job analysis, job description and selection criteria to help you develop your questions. Check your questions against the following which would have produced much better evidence about the interviewee's computer ability. I have left out leading and loaded questions and answering a question with a question, as they seem inappropriate in this situation.

- **Direct:** 'What formulae do you use in your weekly sales report spreadsheet?' 'How would you construct an 'IF' command?'
- **Probing:** 'Why did you say that you prefer Lotus 123 to Excel?'
- **Hypothetical:** 'How would you have gathered information about the hidden people costs if you were unable to contact anyone in the personnel department?'
- **Reflective:** 'You bring things down from the mainframe?'

These questions are likely to yield much more information than Pascale's. Not only do they delve deeper into Juliet's understanding of the topic, but they also require her to have some practical experience to answer them. Although this doesn't conclusively prove that Juliet has the skills about which she speaks, the greater depth should give you more confidence in her ability and this adds to the bigger picture.

Developing interview questions

Refer to the selection criteria for the vacancy you want to fill. Try to think of three questions for each criterion that will help you gather evidence related to it. For each try to imagine how the interviewee will respond. Does the question work? Will it give you the information you need to assess the interviewee's suitability?

Interviewing for organisation fit

Although I specifically separated out job and organisation fit in the early chapters of the book, I merged them when I talked about job descriptions and selection criteria. The purpose of this was to develop a complete and integrated picture of job descriptions and selection criteria. Consequently, if you're in the middle of an organisational entry process and you've produced a set of selection criteria, then in the previous activity you will already have thought about how to ask questions to gather evidence on the applicant's ability to fit into your organisational culture. However, as this is such a new area of interest in selection, it warrants some special attention. How do you go about assessing how well someone will adapt to the environment in which the job is set?

Assessing organisational fit in interviews is difficult. We know from research that one of the prime reasons for using interviews is to assess applicants' fit to the organisation, and that this is commonly done very subjectively. Indeed, if you wanted to reject a candidate simply because you didn't like them, all you have to do is say 'I don't think he'll fit in around here' and then justify it with a few spurious statements. To help you avoid falling into this trap, I will spend some time talking about how you can assess fit to the organisation fairly and accurately.

In chapter 5, I discussed a three stage model of analysis. This model gives you the framework you need to make your organisational fit decisions.

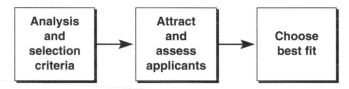

Fig 7.2 A rational selection decision

The idea is that you first determine the nature of the environment in which the job is set and what it takes to thrive in it. You then assess applicants on those characteristics, which are part of your selection criteria, before deciding who best fits the environment. This makes the assessment of organisational fit an objective, systematic, and rational decision making process.

The objective of your questions on organisational fit is to produce evidence regarding:

■ the applicant's environmental preferences
■ how different environments have affected them.

EXAMPLES OF ORGANISATIONAL FIT INTERVIEW QUESTIONS

1 Could you describe the culture of your previous [current] organisation?
[Followed by]
How did [does it] influence your behaviour or actions?
2 Could you compare the culture of the places where you've worked before and how the differences affected your behaviour at work?
3 You don't seem to have enjoyed working at XXXX. What was it about that company that contributed to this feeling?
[or]
You seem to have enjoyed working at XXXX. What was it about that company that contributed to this feeling?
4 Where have you been happiest at work?
[followed by]
What was it about the place that made you feel like this?
5 Can you describe three things that you regretted leaving behind at every company you've worked at?
[and/or]
Can you describe three things that you don't regret leaving behind at every company you've worked at?
6 What do you require from an organisation to get satisfaction from your work?
7 What is the attitude towards conflict [or whatever] where you currently work?
[followed by]
How does this fit in with your attitudes to work?
8 Why did you decide to join each of the organisations you've worked for?
9 What factors will cause you to decide whether or not to leave your current employer?
10 What do you require of an organisation to perform well?
11 Try to think about when you were most unhappy at work. What factors contributed to this?
12 How is your effectiveness measured in your present job?
13 What factors have been important in promotions that you've gained?
14 How do you cope with working in teams [or whatever]?
15 Can you describe the characteristics and nature of your ideal organisation?
16 How does your manager get the best out of you?
17 Could you describe a conducive work atmosphere for me?
18 What type of behaviour at work would raise eyebrows?
19 How will you cope with the change of employer after ... years with your current company?
20 What interests you least about this organisation?

Clearly, you must decide which, if any, of these questions are relevant to your vacancy and each of the candidates. And, most importantly, you should include questions that focus on other specific characteristics of your organisation's environment.

Interviewing checklist

You can use the following checklist to ensure that you and any fellow interviewers are properly prepared for the interview. It has been adapted from Anderson and Shackleton (1993).

THE INTERVIEWING CHECKLIST

Documentary information on the candidate

1 Have all sources of information on the candidate
been received? ❏
  – application form ❏
  – CV ❏
  – test results ❏
  – medical ❏
  – others ❏

2 Have the job description and selection criteria been
scrutinised and understood thoroughly by the interviewers? ❏

3 Have references been received if these were requested in
advance? ❏

4 Has the application been scrutinised to generate question areas? ❏

5 Have important issues for questioning at interview been noted? ❏

Correspondence with the candidate

6 Has the candidate been sent full details of the interview location,
date and time? ❏

7 Has the candidate been provided with a realistic job preview? ❏

8 Has the candidate been informed of the purpose of the interview? ❏

Location and venue

9 Has the interview room been properly set up? ❏

10 Has the receptionist been informed of the applicant's attendance? ❏

11 Have all sources of interruption been eliminated? ❏

Preparation for the interview process

12 Have the structure and format of the interview been
decided upon? ❏

13 If a panel interview is being conducted, has it been agreed which
members of the panel will cover different aspects of the
application? ❏

---

14 Has it been decided how to handle unforeseen areas of
   questioning? ❑
15 Has it been agreed how to answer the candidate's queries and how
   best to provide them with information on the organisation and
   the job applied for? ❑

Decision making procedure and follow-up
16 Has the decision making process been agreed upon? ❑
17 Has it been decided how to close the interview and how to
   structure the candidate's expectations about what happens next? ❑
18 Have all follow-up procedures for correspondence with the
   candidate been decided upon and set up within the organisation? ❑

References
■ ■ ■

Earlier, I said that everything that someone says in an interview
might be false. You get around this by framing questions in such a
manner that only someone with the required skills, knowledge etc. can
answer them. Another way of checking the truth of what the interviewee says is to ask people who should know. This is particularly
important when the person is claiming to have qualifications that are
part of your selection criteria. Unfortunately, it is now very common
for applicants to misrepresent themselves and there are very many
instances of this happening. Taking up references may not be ideal,
but it is a good place to start.

153

The reason for taking up references

References have received quite a bad press over the years. The problem seems related to the fact that recruiting organisations ask applicants to supply the names of two or three referees who then become
champions competing with each other to produce the best possible reference. This appears to happen because referees are asked open questions and to comment on the suitability of a person for a particular
position.

Most referees are truthful and honest and do not want to write misleading or dishonest statements about the candidate. But if you are
vague in your requests for information, the referee will skate over or
avoid things that reflect poorly on the applicant. By agreeing to act as
referees they feel partially responsible for the outcome. So, the referee
asked to produce a reference for someone they know to have faults is
in a dilemma. They want to help the person, but they don't want to

compromise themselves or their organisation. This is a dilemma you can use to your advantage. If you ask the referee direct, closed questions to verify what the candidate has said in the interview, you will almost certainly get straight answers (or no answer, which tells its own story) to your questions.

When interviewing someone for a job, one of your objectives is to gather information or evidence that can be checked. Not only does this help you check its validity, but it also keeps the interviewee on their toes. They will know, more than you, that the information can be checked. This approach reflects well on you and the organisation as you are likely to be perceived as thorough and professional. It might also scare off people who tell stories in the interview.

> **The purpose of references is to verify what the interviewee has said.**

154 | Writing for a reference

When should you write for a reference?

The traditional approach is to send off letters to referees as soon as the applicant is shortlisted, as long as they haven't requested that you don't approach referees until they are to be offered a job. Such is the anxiety surrounding job insecurity these days that this is becoming increasingly common. This traditional approach rather forces you into the problem already described: the problem that reference writing becomes a competition between the champions of applicants. If you follow the alternative approach I've outlined (to verify interview statements), you can only write letters requesting references after the interview. This timing also has the advantage of cutting down on needless administration.

How should you write for a reference?

A letter requesting a reference normally has three parts:

- a short, courteous covering letter explaining who you are and why you are writing
- a short questionnaire
- a self-addressed, prepaid envelope (to make it as easy as possible for the referee to complete the task).

After interviewing the candidate you need to write down all the facts that a referee can verify. If the referee is a previous or current manager, your questionnaire might include questions on the following:

- job title

- duration of employment
- responsibilities
- number of staff supervised
- salary (you will also get confirmation of this when the newcomer joins via the P45)
- courses successfully completed and course content
- money accountable for
- spending power
- promotions.

Make the questionnaire as easy to fill in as possible. Try to use tick boxes and yes/no answers wherever possible.

JOB REFERENCE QUESTIONNAIRE

Jo Bloggs has applied for a job with FizzyPop Limited as a secretary. She has given us your name as a referee. We should be grateful if you would complete this questionnaire and return it to us in the enclosed envelope as soon as possible.

Please verify that the following statements are accurate.

Jo Bloggs has worked as personal assistant to the Managing Director from May 1991 until the present time.   True ❏   False ❏

Jo Bloggs joined the company in August 1987 as a secretary in the marketing department.   True ❏   False ❏

Jo Bloggs is responsible for petty cash.   True ❏   False ❏

Jo Bloggs is highly skilled in the use of Word for Windows.
                                                   True ❏   False ❏

Jo Bloggs supervises and co-ordinates the work of five other secretaries.
                                                   True ❏   False ❏

Jo Bloggs has regular contact with external customers.
                                                   True ❏   False ❏

Jo Bloggs earns £16,000 p.a. plus overtime.
                                                   True ❏   False ❏

Would you like to expand on any of your replies to the above points?

_____
_____
_____
_____

Is there anything else you think we should know about Jo Bloggs?

_____
_____
_____
_____

Form completed by (name and position in BLOCK CAPITALS):

_____

Signature:

_____

Date:

_____

Many thanks for your help. Please return this questionnaire to Rob Kitchen, Personnel Manager, FizzyPop Ltd., FizzyPop House, 111-123 Harrogate Road, York.

Other types of references

There are two other types of reference you should consider. The first concerns other important references that the interviewee has made during the interview. Headhunters follow up all sorts of leads to find the best applicants. You can do the same in reverse. If the applicant says he's worked at the Virgin Megastore on Oxford Street, why not contact them? If she says she has very good contacts with several important customers, why not ask them? There is no reason why you shouldn't research a person more thoroughly if you're intending to offer them a job. However, there are a few questions to which you must be able to answer 'yes' first:

- is it an important factor (i.e. are you taking it into account in deciding whom to offer the job to)?
- is it related to performance at work?
- are you intending to offer the job to the person?
- are you sure that you'll be respecting the applicant's right to confidentiality?

You must not breech these conditions. Furthermore, you should tell the applicant whom you will be approaching and give them the opportunity to veto any approaches. Of course, if they do, you should probe to find out why they object.

The second type of reference you should always carry out is to verify that the applicant holds the qualifications they claim to hold. Universities, colleges, professional institutions, and school examination bodies will all provide copy certificates if requested. Unfortunately, it's unlikely that these bodies will give out information over the phone or to a third party in a letter. You will have to ask the applicant to obtain the relevant certificates and this can take up to a month. If when you see the certificates you're not sure whether they're authentic, you must get in touch with the awarding body to check them. There are regular news items in the media revealing doctors or dentists without qualifications. It is less well known that many people falsely claim to have 'A' levels, a degree, or to be qualified accountants, surveyors or engineers. A delay of a couple of weeks is preferable to being conned by someone who could bring your company considerable trouble.

157

Rejecting candidates

■ ■ ■

Spare a thought for the applicants you reject. Most people put a lot of time and effort into every application. When people get to the interview stage, expectations rise and, if they are rejected, the sense of failure will be even greater. This often translates itself as a loss of self-esteem. Once you receive two or three rejections, it is natural to attribute the failure to your own shortcomings, stupidity or weaknesses. Given the numbers that apply for jobs, this is irrational. But if you've ever been rejected by a couple of organisations, you'll appreciate the feeling. So how should you manage the rejection of applicants?

First, you should be prompt. It is all too common for people to be kept dangling, 'just in case Sara doesn't accept the job'. If an applicant is in this position tell them. And keep them regularly informed about progress.

Second, you should try to make rejection a win/win situation if possible. This may sound fatuous, but it is an important skill. When headhunters have to reject people they've approached, they tend to say that the client wanted a different mix of skills and experience, but that they thought you were very good. There's no reason why you can't adopt a similar approach. But be careful. The more reasons you give for rejection in a letter, the greater the likelihood of comeback. Nowadays, it is more common for rejection letters to be quite short with no reason given for the failure.

Dear Mr Brown,

Re: Purchasing Assistant

Thank you for your recent application for the above post.

I regret to inform you that you have not been shortlisted on this occasion.

Thank you for taking the time and trouble to apply for the post. I hope this rejection will not deter you from making applications in the future.

Yours sincerely,

Robert Lawson

Robert Lawson
Personnel Director

158

Choosing selection techniques

List all the jobs that you might want to fill. Against each one, say which selection techniques you could use to assess candidates. For each selection technique listed, say what quality you hope to test.

SUMMARY – CHAPTER 7 *ASSESSMENT*

- Shortlisting should be done by comparing applicants to the selection criteria in a systematic manner.

- You should choose selection techniques that help you determine which applicants best fit the selection criteria.

- Many selection tests are actually screening tests.

- Screening tests tend to examine very specific qualities. They are best used to ensure that applicants come up to a particular standard on important and relevant details.

- Analogous tests can be particularly useful because they can give applicants a realistic preview of the job as well as examining important qualities.

- Assessment centres are often less useful than the tests they contain because of the problem of combining results.

- Everything that someone says during an interview might be untrue.

- References are used to check that applicants have told you the truth.

- You should always check any certificates and qualifications that applicants claim to have.

8

■ ■ ■

How do you determine terms and conditions?

CHAPTER OBJECTIVES

After reading this chapter you should be able to:
- define the term 'psychological contract'
- describe how psychological contracts are formed
- appreciate the impact of your actions upon the subsequent performance and morale of the newcomer
- negotiate terms and conditions with applicants so that both sides win
- write an offer letter
- make up a welcome pack.

CHAPTER OVERVIEW

New employees have two contracts. Everyone knows about the first; the formal contract of employment that sets out roles, duties, responsibilities, grievance procedures, health and safety matters, notice periods, holiday entitlement and so on. This is a vital document with legal implications for both employee and employer. Not many people know about the second type of contract. This is a psychological contract between the employee and the employer. It is rarely written down or discussed, but it is just as important as the first, probably more so because the psychological contract influences the behaviour of both parties. It is important in organisational entry because many of your words and actions during the process will have a significant effect on shaping the psychological contracts of newcomers. Towards the end of the selection process, the objective of the interviewer changes, and the focus is much more on negotiating or agreeing contracts of employment, both formal and psychological. In this chapter, I look at this critical stage of organisational entry – between selection and the start of work – as there is much you can do to shape the contracts of employment to the benefit of both parties.

Psychological contracts

■ ■ ■

Organisational entry isn't just about **finding** the *right* people. It's also about **motivating** the *right* people. This might sound a little strange. I can hear you saying 'how can organisational entry motivate employees?'

Can organisational entry motivate people?

Can you describe the selection process you went through to get your current job?

In what ways did you feel differently about the job at the end of the process?

Most people find that the selection process changes the way they think about the job they're about to do, albeit very subtly. How would you react if the person interviewing you was completely disorganised, hadn't read your CV, didn't look you in the eye, and didn't give you the chance to ask questions? What if the person interviewing you cracks racist and sexist jokes? If they don't appear very bright? If they're desperate to recruit you? What impression would you get? On the other hand, if the interviewer was friendly, welcoming, considerate and so on, how would you feel about the organisation? Given that this is a time in your life when you dwell on every scrap of information and you usually have four or five weeks uncertainty before you can check your assumptions, these impressions tend to get blown out of all proportion and shape your attitudes towards your employer. But the manner of the selection process is only half the story. The content is also very important, because the discussions between you and the interviewer shape your expectations about the job, informing you about what the organisation expects of you and vice versa. It is these discussions and negotiations that can affect your motivation, commitment, and satisfaction.

What is a psychological contract?

Because it is all about psychological issues, it is often not stated; many of the issues making up a psychological contract may not be consciously known to either side. For example, an employee might require their boss to talk to them before changes occur. But this is the sort of

> **A PSYCHOLOGICAL CONTRACT is the employee's [or employer's] understanding of what their employer [or employee] expects of them and what they will get in return.**

thing that doesn't get discussed during organisational entry. How could the discussion cover the thousands of items of concern to both parties? As a result, much of the psychological contract is unspoken, taken for granted, and assumed from more general discussion.

The psychological contract is important because it influences behaviours and attitudes to work. It influences how people go about their work. Research has shown that *greater agreement* between employee and employer on the nature of the psychological contract leads to *greater* job satisfaction, productivity, ethical behaviour, trainee satisfaction, and reduced turnover of staff. It is the agreement between the two parties that is important, not the components of the agreement. Clearly then, the psychological contract is important and needs to be managed if possible.

162

Your expectations

What do you contribute at work (e.g. time, effort)?

What do you expect in return from your employer?

Either   a) What could your employer do to improve your level of contribution?

Or   b) What would your employer have to do to reduce your level of contribution?

The purpose of this exercise is to illustrate the complex nature of the psychological contract. At work we contribute all manner of things. Examples would be time, effort, attention to detail, our positive attitude when talking to customers, willingness to contribute ideas, co-operative behaviour. This is partly from fear of losing our job or chances of promotion, and also because we are professional people. But the quality of work is also influenced by more subtle things controlled by the organisation. Little things such as locking the stationery cupboard after ten o'clock, or changing the allocation of space or location of the department in the building (which are rarely in contracts of employment or discussed during organisational entry) can really get under people's skin and lead to less effort, less willingness to work longer hours and so on. Think about the variations in the way you do things. What causes these variations?

How do psychological contracts form?

How did you form your opinions and attitudes towards your employer? There is no simple answer. You interact with a large number of people, sometimes in formal settings, sometimes very informally. All sorts of situations inform you about the expectations of the organisation. Who gets promoted? What sort of training is offered? How are performance reviews carried out? What do people talk about over the photocopier or in the pub after work? The employee's side of the psychological contract forms as a result of the myriad of major and minor interactions that they have with the organisation. All these inform the individual of what the organisation expects of them.

The interactions split into two types: formal and informal. The organisation has very little control, if any, over the informal interactions. But it can control the formal interactions, to some extent. Amongst these are training, pay, performance reviews, promotion and so on. The manner of these represents a choice by the organisation as to how it wishes to treat people. And, of course, one of the most important interactions that the organisation can control is organisational entry.

163

Organisational entry is particularly important because when people change employers, they join the company desperately seeking to make sense of the new environment. It is a time of great uncertainty when new ideas have more prominence than usual. New ideas can crystallise at this time and become the new employee's set way of thinking about and relating to their new employer. You need to ensure that you communicate the right message to applicants so that they join fully aware of what the organisation will expect of them.

Can you manage psychological contracts?

Obviously you cannot control what people think. You wouldn't want to and it wouldn't be right to try. But you can give them the information they need to make up their own minds. What information is this? There is one cardinal rule: people need accurate and realistic information. I said earlier that the most important aspect of the psychological contract was the degree of agreement between employee and employer. As in most cases, there is little the organisation can do to change its expectations of its employees, it is usually up to the newcomer to change and adapt to the organisation. To do this, they need to know what it is like to work at the organisation and what the organisation will expect of them.

> **Potential employees need accurate and realistic information about what the organisation will expect of them.**

You can do several things to manage the information that applicants receive. Earlier in the book I talked about the importance of realistic advertisements and realistic job previews. It is difficult to understate their importance. Not only do they help shape the psychological contracts of new recruits, they also help many people realise that the organisation is not for them. You can also do several other things to improve the information flows to applicants.

- Organisational entry processes should be a reflection of behaviour and practices in the organisation. If you dress them up and make the process unlike life in the organisation, the applicant will get no impression, or the wrong impression, of what work will be like. This point mainly refers to the manner or atmosphere of the process. Time and again, research has shown that tone is more important than content in effective communication.

- As you want to help applicants understand the organisation's expectations, it follows that your delivery must be clear and truthful.

- Interviewers often 'talk up' the job to encourage people to pursue their application. This misleads the applicant, which is unfortunate because employee and employer need to come to a mutual agreement about what each party expects of the other. Therefore, you need to talk with the applicant, not at them. This is important after the person has joined, as well as during recruitment and selection.

164

> **Talk *with* the applicant, not *at* them.**

Negotiations
■ ■ ■

Towards the end of the selection process, time is normally set aside to negotiate with the applicant. Typically this happens at the end of a second interview. Questions like 'how much would you expect to be paid?' and 'when could you start?' are the opening shots in the negotiation. More sophisticated negotiations can involve a supposedly neutral intermediary such as a headhunter.

The agreement or negotiation period in organisational entry is commonly performed very poorly. One reason for this is that participants can easily fall into the trap of trying to win the negotiation at the expense of the other party. This is ill-advised for two reasons:

- one of the objectives of organisational entry is to build a strong relationship between the two parties where both stand to benefit by helping each other
- it is likely to be a self-defeating strategy as the losing party can dig its heels in and walk away from the negotiation.

These reasons highlight the three possible outcomes of conflict and negotiation situations:

- **Win-win.** Both sides come out having benefited from the negotiation.
- **Win-lose.** One side wins at the expense of the other. An example would be an organisation recruiting someone on a salary well below the market rate or below what people doing similar jobs in the organisation are earning. What is the likely outcome of this situation? It doesn't take a genius to realise that the newcomer is likely to be less than delighted which might lead to lower motivation, poorer performance, and dissatisfaction. There will be continual pressure for reassessment, heightened levels of conflict, and perhaps the decision to leave the company. All of these feelings might spread to other workers. This illustrates a problem common in organisational entry situations: win-lose solutions are usually lose-lose situations.
- **Lose-lose.** Both sides lose. This is all too common in organisational entry. It usually results in a recruited person leaving or a mutual decision to go their separate ways before the job is offered.

165

Getting to win-win

There are two approaches to negotiation:

- **Distributive** bargaining. This occurs when there is a fixed amount of something to win. So, if I gain more, you lose some. It is a zero-sum game.
- **Integrative** bargaining. This occurs when the prize can be shared and we can both benefit. We can get to a win-win situation.

Clearly, organisational entry is a game with a possible win-win prize. You want to recruit someone with certain skills. The candidate has applied because they want the job you offer. In organisational entry there are levels of win-win. The basic win-win was just described. But this can be enhanced, if the newcomer joins with heightened motivation, or if they get greater satisfaction from their work. In many circumstances, you want to recruit someone who can develop and grow within the organisation, gain promotions and so on. Usually, the applicant also hopes this will happen.

To help you get to win-win you can use a simplified model of the negotiation process developed by Robbins (1996):

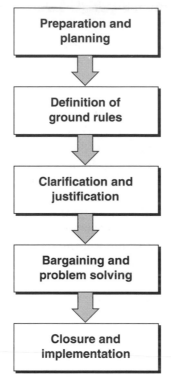

Fig 8.1 The negotiation process

The negotiation process has five stages:

■ **Preparation and planning.** What is the nature of the negotiation you are about to enter? What do you want to achieve? What
are the other party's goals?

■ **Definition of ground rules.** Where will the negotiation be held? Will there be an intermediary? Are there any time constraints? Are there any subjects you don't want to cover?

■ **Clarification and justification.** Each party needs to be open about its objectives, position, expectations, arguments and so on. All cards should be on the table. If cards are hidden, one of the players is aiming for win-lose.

■ **Bargaining and problem solving.** Try to find the best mutually beneficial solution. You can use the rational decision making model described earlier. Five guidelines can help you negotiate to better advantage:
  – begin with a positive overture
  – address problems, not personalities
  – pay little attention to initial offers
  – emphasise win-win solutions
  – create an open and trusting climate.

■ **Closure and implementation.** Formalise the agreement that you have reached. Write it down. Check that both agree that it fairly represents the agreement. Agree the implementation plan. How will it be monitored?

NEGOTIATION GUIDELINES

1 Begin with a positive overture.
2 Address problems, not personalities.
3 Pay little attention to initial offers.
4 Emphasise win-win solutions.
5 Create an open and trusting climate.

Is integrative bargaining realistic?

To many people, the above model seems idealistic and unrealistic. What do you think?

● In the past have you tried to achieve win-win solutions?
● If not, what stops you from trying to achieve a win-win solution?
● What do you think would be the advantages if you adopted an integrative approach to negotiation in organisational entry?

What can stop you getting to win-win?

Adopting an integrative approach is far from easy. For many people, it cuts across years of managerial experience and training. Managers are employed to get the best deal for the organisation. The integrative approach doesn't contradict this legitimate response. But it does suggest that there is a better outcome than getting a new recruit at the lowest possible cost, or whatever.

In the vast majority of situations, managers hold more power than applicants. They make the ultimate decision of whether to employ the person, how much to pay them and so on. They have interviewed seven or eight other applicants, some of whom would be perfectly acceptable, and failed to shortlist a hundred or more other candidates. They know they have options.

Applicants are in a much weaker situation. It might be the first interview they've had after 50 applications. They might be desperate to leave their current employer. They might be desperate for a job. It takes a strong manager to put their cards on the table and reject their power in favour of coming to a mutually beneficial agreement that values partnership above exploitation. You will only be prepared to do this if you genuinely believe in the benefits to the organisation.

The value of staff

Pick a member of your current staff.

- How much do they cost to employ?
- What is the same person's worth to the organisation?

> *The purpose of this reflective exercise is to illustrate a trend in management towards short term actions. Such is the pressure on managers that we all tend to focus on the short term costs rather than the long term value or worth. Nowhere is this more evident than in organisational entry. It is relatively easy to quantify what people cost to employ, but quite difficult to quantify their value or worth to the firm.*

Offer letters
■ ■ ■

The offer letter is a vitally important document. Not only does it have legal implications, it also informs the person that they have been successful in their application and deemed good enough to become a 'member of the club'. As such it should congratulate the person. The offer letter is urgent as well as important, because it is usually the trigger for the successful applicant to resign from their current job. Time wasted in sending out the offer letter is likely to delay the starting date of the newcomer.

When would you resign?

Imagine that you were applying for a job at another organisation. Under what circumstances would you resign before receiving the offer letter?

This simple reflection illustrates the importance of the offer letter. It has to be quite extraordinary circumstances for someone to resign before receiving it.

The offer letter should confirm the agreement made during the negotiation phase of the process and shouldn't be written if anything has yet to be settled. The two exceptions to this rule are if you are waiting for satisfactory references (including certificate checks) or a satisfactory medical check. If either are applicable, you should make it clear in the letter that the offer is conditional on these matters being successfully completed.

You will probably want to include the following in your offer letter:

- job title
- a brief job description including grade (with explanation)
- lines of report
- starting date
- length of contract and termination conditions
- period of notice
- hours of work
- holidays
- location
- relocation arrangements (if appropriate)
- starting salary, method of payment, and arranged increases
- other benefits
- sick pay and sick leave
- pension arrangements
- probationary period.

169

The offer letter doesn't need to include a contract of employment although a contract exists as soon as the newcomer accepts the offer of work in return for pay. You have 13 weeks to provide the new employee with a contract of employment. You will probably already have these in your organisation. If not, then you might want to get legal advice before drawing one up.

An example of an offer letter follows. It relates to an internal promotion within a hotel. It illustrates how to write a letter for a fixed period contract.

[on a company letterhead]

PERSONAL AND CONFIDENTIAL

[date]
[name and address]

Dear Ms Turner,

Following your recent interview, I am pleased to offer you a temporary three year appointment with Scottish Hotels Ltd. as Manager with duties in the Stirling Scottish Hotel, Stirling at a salary of £23,000 per annum, which will be paid by monthly bank credit in arrears. The salary scale appropriate to your grade (S) is from £18,000 to £35,000 per annum. Your first increment will take effect from 1st April 1996. You will be responsible initially to the Regional Director (East Scotland), who is located in the company's Edinburgh office.

We would like you to take up this appointment on 1st January 1996.

For statutory purposes your continuous employment dates from 25th May 1990.

The full conditions of appointment are as given in the terms and conditions for full-time managerial staff which you currently hold. Your attention is drawn to paragraph 40 (Duties) and in particular that you will be required to undertake such other duties as may be assigned by your supervisor from time to time in furtherance of the company's objectives. The company reserves the right to make changes to your duties and to require you to work in other areas of the company and be subject to any special conditions applying in those areas. Provisions for notice are set out in paragraph 38. The appointment is terminable by six months notice in writing on either side.

Failing prior termination or renewal, the appointment will expire on 31st December 1998. It is a condition of this contract of employment that you agree to exclude in the event of the expiry of the term of this employment without it being renewed:

> any claim in respect of rights under Section 54 of the Employment Protection (Consolidation) Act 1978, or any statutory modification or re-enactment thereof.

> This clause waives your right to claim unfair dismissal when the contract ceases on the expiry date as stated above.

The probationary period will not apply to this post.

If you are prepared to accept this offer on the terms and conditions stated, please sign the additional copy of this letter and return it in the envelope provided.

Congratulations on your appointment.

Yours sincerely,

Michael Cook
Human Resource Director
for and on behalf of
Scottish Hotels Ltd.

Welcome packs
■ ■ ■

Many organisations choose to separate the offer letter from the welcome pack. In most circumstances this is quite wise. You want the offer letter to be highly visible and it can get lost in the multitude of things commonly sent to newcomers before they join. The decision to put together a separate welcome pack also helps you to tailor it to your specific requirements.

Welcome packs can be put together in very different ways to reflect different concerns. Typically these include:

- to inform newcomers of legal considerations
- to excite newcomers
- to deal with the administration of joining
- to reduce the anxiety and stress of joining (more on this in the next chapter).

The objective is usually a mixture of all of the above, even though this amalgamation tends to dilute the message. Typically, a welcome pack will include the following:

171

- a letter informing the newcomer of the purpose of the welcome pack and a checklist of things they must do before they arrive
- instructions of whom, where and when to report to on their first day of work
- instructions of what to bring along on their first day of work
- a cheery welcome letter from the chief executive or equivalent
- terms and conditions of employment
- an introductory letter from the recognised trade union or staff association (if appropriate)
- details of pension arrangements
- a realistic preview of the job
- staff manuals containing organisation charts, biographies of people they'll be working closely with, office plans, company history, products and services, training opportunities and so on.

In addition, there is a range of things that you might want to request in the welcome pack to save time on the first day:

- clothing size for uniform purchase
- computer specification
- holidays already booked
- relocation details.

The welcome pack should tell newcomers what to bring along on their first day. You might want to include:

- P45 or National Insurance number
- SSP forms
- bank or building society details
- birth certificate or passport
- work permit
- driving licence
- photographs
- completed forms (medical questionnaire, car parking form, security card request, pension forms etc.).

Pre-introduction checklist

You can use the following checklist to ensure that you are ready for the newcomer's first day. It has been adapted from Skeats (1991).

Some of the subjects mentioned in the checklist, such as buddies, mentors, and stress reduction programmes, might be unfamiliar. They are discussed in the next two chapters.

SUMMARY - CHAPTER 8 *AGREEMENT*

- A psychological contract is the unwritten, informal agreement between employee and employer about what each party expects of the other and what each party expects to contribute to the other.

- Potential employees need accurate and realistic information about what the organisation will expect of them.

- Talk with the applicant, not at them.

- Organisational entry is a win-win situation.

- Offer letters should congratulate the newcomer.

- Offer letters are legally binding on the organisation.

- Offer letters are urgent.

- Welcome packs are used to:
  - inform newcomers of legal considerations
  - excite newcomers
  - deal with the administration of joining
  - reduce the anxiety and stress of joining.

THE PRE-INTRODUCTION CHECKLIST

The offer letter
1 Has the offer letter been sent? ❑
2 Has the acceptance been received? ❑

The welcome pack
3 Have joining instructions been issued? ❑
  – reporting instructions – to whom, where, what time ❑
  – transport routes and maps ❑
  – request to bring certain information – e.g. P45, photographs ❑
4 Has the welcome pack been sent? ❑
5 Have you received any requested material? ❑

Administration
6 Have you (or the relevant manager) put aside time on the
  morning of the newcomer's first day to talk to them? ❑
7 Have you (or the relevant manager) organised work for the
  newcomer's first day? ❑
8 Has the previous job holder been asked to leave notes about
  the job? ❑
9 Has the office space/desk/locker etc. been cleaned, prepared,
  and equipped? ❑
10 Have security passes, nameplate, business cards, computer
  passwords/access, cash floats, keys etc. been ordered or
  authorised for the newcomer? ❑
11 Is the introduction programme arranged? ❑
12 Have all the participants in the introduction programme agreed
  on the approach, rehearsed, and blocked out time in their diaries? ❑
13 Do you (or the relevant manager) need to arrange refresher
  training on how to coach/train? ❑
14 Has the newcomer been booked on to an induction course
  (if one is not being prepared specially) and any other agreed
  training programmes? ❑
15 Has an anxiety or stress reduction programme been organised? ❑
16 Has a buddy or mentor been chosen and briefed? ❑
17 Have the post room and switchboard been told the
  newcomer's name, job title, date of arrival, room number
  and telephone number? ❑
18 Have other people been told when the newcomer is arriving
  and who they are? ❑

9

■ ■ ■

Surviving the first day

CHAPTER OBJECTIVES

After reading this chapter you should be able to:
- describe how stressful starting a new job can be
- develop a basic anxiety and stress reduction programme
- manage a newcomer's first day at work.

CHAPTER OVERVIEW

Many organisations have developed very good formal induction courses for newcomers, which can help the newcomer adapt to their new environment. However, I do not discuss these types of induction course in this book. There are many good books on this subject and the focus of this book is what individuals can do to be effective at organisational entry. So, I concentrate on what the individual manager or department head can do themselves to help introduce the newcomer into the organisation. This splits into two sections. First, those activities you can arrange to ease the anxiety and stress of joining a new organisation. Second, the important but mundane and administrative things you can do to ease the newcomer into their work so that they become effective as quickly as possible.

Anxiety and stress reduction
■ ■ ■

Introduction is the initial period of employment when the newcomer is adjusting to the new environment. This period is also referred to as induction and orientation. The period of newcomer induction varies, but is usually between a day and a week in length. During this period, newcomers are concerned about the expectations the organisation has of them, meeting strangers with whom they must form working relationships, loneliness, using new technology and being able to do the job. This can cause great anxiety and even stress which is potentially unhealthy and unproductive. The purpose of organisational induction programmes is to reduce the stress associated with changing environments. I use the term 'introduction' to highlight the need to help the newcomer on and before the first day of employment.

Good introduction is particularly important for organisational entry processes that have not addressed the issue of developing a psychological contract or included a realistic preview or description of the role. In these cases, anxiety is intensified as the newcomer arrives having no idea what is expected of them.

175

How serious is newcomer stress?

There have been several studies of newcomer stress. One study examined army recruits entering basic training. The researchers found that anxiety and stress levels were at their highest on the first day. They analysed blood and urine samples and found that levels of chemicals associated with extreme high stress were comparable to those found in mental patients in hospital.

Why are anxiety and stress levels so high at this time? One explanation is that newcomers have to undergo 'multiple role transitions'. Not only does the person have to adapt to changes at work, but usually a change of job affects other issues outside work. A good example of this is a school leaver getting their first full-time job. Not only do they have to change from being a student to a worker, but they might have to move away from home for the first time, they start earning, they have to manage domestically, they will lose friends, gain others, and so on. This is even more common for graduates.

How did your life change?

Think back to when you joined your current organisation. How did your life change?

> *For most people, the start of a new job is one of the most significant role transitions in their lives. They have to establish new friendships and new working relationships. A job change may present a newcomer with a new set of tasks to be mastered. They may be a little unsure of what is expected of them. A new job may necessitate a house move – another stressful event – and there may be associated changes for a partner or children. These factors combine to make starting a new job one of the most stressful events in a person's life.*

176

When Juliet decided to work for the building society, she made a decision that changed her life and the lives of members of her family. Previously she had been working in the accounts department of a large high street department store. The work had been fairly routine and there were few opportunities for growth and development. The people made the job bearable. But Juliet wanted more of a challenge and that prompted her to contact the agency.

Although the building society wasn't very far from home, the journey to work meant travelling into the centre of London and back out on the tube. This added about forty minutes to her journey time. Just this relatively small change had a significant effect. Her two young children had to be taken to the child-minder forty minutes earlier and normally weren't picked up until after six in the evening. When she was home, Juliet had much less time with them and everything became rushed. She would pick up the children on the way home. By the time she had fed them, played with them, put them to bed and cleared up, it was late. Most nights, Juliet wouldn't get any peace and quiet until 9.30. And she now had to go to bed earlier, to get up earlier, to get to work.

Was it worth moving house to be closer to work? There would be considerable advantages, but she was living with negative equity and the upheavals associated with moving would be most disrupting and time consuming. Besides, she had friends in the area and she didn't want the hassle of finding and vetting a new child-minder.

On top of it all, Juliet wasn't enjoying her work and wasn't sure how long she'd stay at her new company. Her boss, Pascale, was nowhere to be seen and everyone in the department seemed to hate her. There was none of the community spirit that there had been in the department store. At times she thought there was a conspiracy not to talk to her. She had already been back in touch with the agency pleading to be rescued from the hell she was working in.

The topics of anxiety and stress have attracted a lot of research, which has revealed that moderate levels can contribute to high performance, but too much results in poor performance. Perhaps more important for organisational entry is the research finding concerning the connection of high anxiety and stress to low job satisfaction.

> **The first few days and weeks of employment are a key period when impressions and expectations are being formed. Low levels of job satisfaction experienced at this time might crystallise and become part of the newcomer's fixed attitudes regarding the job and the organisation.**

John Wanous has developed some general guidelines that will help you to design anxiety and stress reduction programmes for newcomers.

- **Include realistic information** – this is an extension of the realistic job preview. Newcomers need to know exactly what they are expected to do and how to do it. This stage should include all of the information that they need (such as whom to ask questions of) to carry out the work effectively.
- **Provide general support and reassurance.**
- **Use models to show coping skills** – Wanous suggests that 'it is insufficient just to talk about how to cope. Newcomers must see some sort of 'model' actually performing the recommended actions to solve or prevent certain [...] stressors.' In short, you should show newcomers how others have coped with the transition they're about to go through.
- **Discuss the model's actions.**
- **Rehearse** – once you have decided upon your anxiety and stress reduction scheme, you need to run through it to make sure it works. This is true for your entire organisational entry programme.
- **Teach self-control of thoughts and feelings** – as it is impossible to demonstrate how to cope with all situations that might arise, newcomers need some general techniques to help them cope with anxiety and stress, such as relaxation techniques.

- **Target specific stressors to specific newcomers** – different jobs generate different types and forms of stress. It is important that you take account of this when recruiting.

Designing an anxiety and stress reduction programme

- What information needs to be communicated?
- What support and reassurance can be offered?
- Who can be used as models?
- Discuss models' actions
- Who needs to rehearse?
- What self-control methods can you teach?
- How does this vacancy differ to others?

To demonstrate how you might do this, here is a possible plan of action for the job of the finance clerk you met earlier.

- Once the formalities of entry are finished, the newcomer would be introduced to their work station, shown the basics and given whatever training was required to do the job. This would remove some of the uncertainty associated with the change of job and help the newcomer control their thoughts and feelings. The new finance clerk would be introduced to people in the department and reassured that help was close at hand.

- On this first day, the newcomer would be encouraged to speak to several other people who had joined recently to discuss how they had coped with the adaptation. Just because this programme is geared to one specific new entrant rather than a large number of entrants, it is no excuse not to rehearse the orientation programme.

- All those involved would have a meeting about a week before the newcomer's start date to discuss the itinerary and each person's role in the process. At this meeting, it is stressed that an important outcome of the introduction programme is that the newcomer feels that they can come to any of the participants for help, advice, or just a chat. In addition, all participants block out time in their diaries to meet the newcomer.

> **These general guidelines are useful for designing basic anxiety or stress reduction programmes. However, if you intend to develop anything more elaborate I would strongly recommend that you seek the advice of a qualified expert as this will be a major psychological intervention.**

Finally, it needs reiterating that introduction involves the reduction of anxiety and stress when entering a new organisation. Programmes designed to reduce this anxiety and stress should be applied in the newcomer's first week of employment, preferably on the first day of employment. There is no reason why stress reduction programmes cannot be applied before the newcomer joins the organisation; it is simple enough to design and produce material that gives newcomers a realistic preview of what their first day will be like. This material could incorporate short case studies, examples of successful and unsuccessful coping strategies, descriptions of the culture and so on. One cause of anxiety is the unknown. Such material could be sent out a couple of weeks before the newcomer joins with the 'welcome pack', and this would help to reduce the unknown element of starting a new job. The teaching technology used by quality distance learning organisations such as the Open University or the Open College could act as an excellent model for the design of an introduction or welcome pack.

The first day of employment
■ ■ ■

First days are important and can shape attitudes towards work. To illustrate this point, have a go at the following exercises which ask you to think about your first day with your current employer.

Your first day (1)

Think back to your first day at your current organisation. What do you remember about it? What opinions did you form about your employer? How have they changed?

> First days tend to be remembered. My very first day at work after leaving university was at a small independent record company in the Midlands. It just happened that it was the managing director's birthday. It was party time. The morning was birthday cake and champagne. Lunch was a fancy restaurant. And the afternoon was very short (everyone was so inebriated). I formed the opinion of a fun company where everyone was on first name terms and enjoyed life. And, to a large extent, this was a true reflection of the place. However, amongst all the revelry, it was clear that the managing director dominated the company and there was an element of fear in the atmosphere. It was a cult of personality. For me, this became unbearable after a year and a half and caused me to leave.

> *The purpose of this reflective exercise is to highlight the effect that first days have on people. Newcomers are desperately looking for something to grab hold off to make sense of their new surroundings. Ideas formed at this time take on a disproportionately strong weighting and may shape the employee's attitude to work.*

Your first day (2)

Again, think back to your first day with your current employer. When you went to work that day, can you remember what your concerns were?

> *Generally speaking, newcomers are concerned about four things:*
>
> - *what will the people be like?*
> - *what will I be expected to do?*
> - *what will the place be like?*
> - *what will the organisation be like?*
>
> *Did you mention any of these? Underpinning these questions is a large number of other concerns. Can I do the job? Have I really got the skills they want? Will I be lonely? Who can I trust? What if I can't get on with anyone? What will my boss really be like? Will I understand the jargon? Should I wear a suit?*

180

I've already discussed how for some people uncertainty about these unknown factors can raise considerable anxiety. And how realistic previews of the job and anxiety and stress reduction programmes can help the newcomer cope. The objective of the following section is to look at the practical things you can do on the first day (other than anxiety and stress reduction programmes) to ease the newcomer into the job and the organisation.

The first moments

Before the newcomer joins the organisation, you can't be sure whether they have prepared themselves for the transition. But in the opening moments of the first day you can control everything that happens. You can remove some of the uncertainty in the newcomer's mind and demonstrate the professional nature of your organisation. There are several simple things you can do to improve the newcomer's first day experience.

- Check that the receptionist, security guards etc. know that the person is joining, know the person's name, and to whom they should report. Ideally, the newcomer should be accompanied rather than directed to their manager or supervisor. It is of considerable benefit if the people greeting the newcomer have a cheery disposition and welcome the newcomer. But you may not have any control over this.

- You should meet your new charge and spend as much time with them as required to explain their new job. This will probably include discussions of how it fits into the objectives and structure of the organisation, how performance will be assessed, probationary periods, lines of report, who to ask for training or coaching (and buddying and mentoring if applicable), and, all importantly, the information they require on how to do their job.

- You should introduce the newcomer to their colleagues. If people are out of the office, book a time with them. It is important that existing workers know of the arrival of the newcomer and the nature of their job beforehand. Not only does this save embarrassment, and help you prearrange what people will talk about (such as what they do and how the newcomer will interact with them), but it also helps existing staff cope with the change themselves. *Obviously, you will have had meetings with existing staff to explain the nature of the change well in advance of the new person starting.*

181

- You should take the person to the personnel department to complete the formalities of joining. Company handbooks, health and safety issues, uniforms, issues keys and passes, cash advances against salary, company cars, and confidentiality matters are usually sorted out at this time. Some organisations ask the newcomer to report to personnel before meeting the manager. You should check procedures in your organisation before arranging times for people to meet the newcomer.

- Arrange for someone, or yourself, to take the newcomer to lunch. A lonely hour in the middle of the day to mull over the experience can be most disconcerting and should be avoided at all costs.

All of these things should be prearranged and no one the newcomer meets should be surprised by their presence. Existing staff should know why the newcomer is there, what their job will be, and why they are meeting them.

If you fail to prepare, you prepare to fail!

Later on

Once the newcomer's quietly getting on with their job, your job's not over. You'd probably want to check things are going well in the early afternoon. In addition, you should arrange a time towards the end of the first day to discuss how things have gone, whether the newcomer's expectations were met, if there's anything they need to help them be more effective and so on. Two further timetabled meetings, one at the start of work on the second morning and one towards the end of the first week, are also very useful. Even if there's nothing to be discussed, it shows you care and are someone they can turn to if they experience problems.

In this first week, you should also quietly and discretely monitor the reactions of existing members of staff. How are they adapting to the change? How is their work being affected?

SUMMARY - CHAPTER 9 *ADJUSTMENT*

- Introduction takes place on, or before, the newcomer's first day at work

- Newcomers can experience considerable role transition when they start a new job.

- Introduction is a key period when impressions and expectations are being formed. Low levels of job satisfaction experienced at this time might crystallise and become part of the newcomer's fixed attitudes regarding the job and the organisation.

- Anxiety and stress reduction programmes should:
  - include realistic information
  - provide general support and reassurance
  - use models to show coping skills
  - discuss the model's actions
  - be rehearsed
  - teach self-control of thoughts and feelings
  - target specific stressors to specific newcomers.

- A newcomer's first day at work should be fully prepared and managed.

- No one the newcomer meets on the first day should be surprised to see them.

- Build time into your diary for meetings with the newcomer to monitor how they are adapting to the new environment.

10
■ ■ ■

Becoming effective as quickly as possible

CHAPTER OBJECTIVES

After reading this chapter you should be able to:
- describe why it is important to consider socialisation for newcomers
- organise effective buddying and mentoring of newcomers.

CHAPTER OVERVIEW

It's very tempting to think that once you've recruited someone and got them settled down to work organisational entry is over. Unfortunately this isn't the case. For the newcomer the adventure is just starting. They may be sitting at their desk beavering away, but inside they're a turmoil of confusion, anxiety, and uncertainty. What should I be trying to achieve here? What does my boss really want of me? How should I behave in meetings? Can I really go to my boss with problems? Should I bawl people out if they don't perform? Why do we have to pay for coffee? In this chapter, I concentrate on the adaptation stage of organisational entry: socialisation. The goal of socialisation is to help the newcomer understand the values of the organisation; if they understand these, they are more likely to adopt behaviour and make decisions in line with the organisation's values. In this chapter, I look at two socialisation techniques that are particularly relevant to newcomers: buddying and mentoring. I end by looking very briefly at personalisation which is the adaptation of the organisation to the newcomer.

Socialisation

■ ■ ■

Socialisation is the adaptation of the newcomer to the organisation. Therefore, introduction is a specific socialisation process that deals explicitly with anxiety, stress, and surviving the first day. I have separated it from other socialisation functions because it has a special time schedule and a specific focus. However, it is inevitable that the approach taken to reduce anxiety is implicitly tied in with organisational values and therefore helps the newcomer to identify with and adapt to these.

Is socialisation important?

As already stated, when people join a new organisation they are subject to a great deal of change and adaptation in their lives. This can be minimised by trying to select people who will fit the environment. But no one fits perfectly, and some adaptation is always necessary. And some people are more adaptable than others. Those that cannot adapt tend to leave and this has unfortunate consequences for all concerned. This cycle of events was addressed by an American psychologist and researcher, Ben Schneider. He argued that organisations are functions of the kinds of people they contain and that organisations attract, select and then keep people who share their values. He termed this the ASA (attraction-selection-attrition) cycle. Consequently, he argues that organisations seek 'right types' when they recruit; i.e. people who share the same attitudes. This, he says, is dysfunctional as there is a danger that organisational cultures and climates will be preserved at a time of increasing change in the wider environment. This highlights the delicate balance that you face during organisational entry: you want to locate people who can thrive and perform in the culture, but at the same time you want to attract people with new and innovative ideas.

Socialisation is important because you want new recruits to identify with the values of the organisation. The idea underpinning this is that closer alignment of individual and organisational values will result in individuals adopting behaviour consistent with the values of the organisation. As such, socialisation might be considered a control mechanism that promotes conformity. This has led some writers (and even more employees) to assert that socialisation is simply another name for brainwashing. Although socialisation will not be acceptable to many, research has shown that greater alignment to the values and norms of the organisation is highly correlated to greater satisfaction, commitment and performance, and lower levels of staff turnover.

How can you help socialisation along?

Socialisation is a process of change. It is a process that has no definite end as it continues throughout a person's employment. It begins the moment an individual becomes interested in joining your organisation, sometimes even earlier if your organisation is well known, as the individual's expectations are formed and shaped by everything they find out about it.

The values and norms where you work

How did you find out about the values and norms of your current employer? What socialisation techniques and events were most effective in communicating them to you?

It is impossible to guess how you might have answered the question: there is an infinite number of socialisation techniques and events that you might have mentioned. The common theme is that they all convey information about the organisation and what people in it value. Whether it is the casual conversation in the pub with a colleague, a formal induction course, or an event such as an appraisal interview, they all give you the information you need to make sense of your surroundings.

Socialisation techniques

On entry, socialisation occurs in all activities and situations. This might be termed a period of social learning. Some activities and situations are more influential than others at socialising. Good examples are:

- many basic training activities
- participation on project teams and group work in general
- mentoring and buddying schemes
- experience-based approaches such as visits
- simulations
- role plays.

Most of these speak for themselves, but a couple, buddying and mentoring, deserve special mention as you may be unaware of what each involves.

Buddying

Despite its appalling name, buddying can be a very valuable early socialisation technique. Buddying is simply pairing up the newcomer with another employee, usually someone who will work closely with them. The buddy should be a good role model and someone who can understand the problems that the newcomer might be facing. The opportunity to talk to a sympathetic buddy can help the newcomer better understand their job, help them cope with the anxiety of joining as there is always someone to turn to for advice, and avoid the loneliness of changing jobs.

There are also advantages for the buddy. Being a buddy is likely to increase their self-esteem and make them feel more responsible and more trusted. Helping the newcomer make sense of the organisation's values and norms gives them the opportunity to think about these issues themselves. Buddying can also be a useful way of identifying supervisory talent.

Mentoring

186

A mentor is a person a new employee can approach for advice. Mentoring differs from buddying in that the mentor is usually a more experienced and more senior employee who is knowledgeable about life in the organisation. They are available to offer a word of advice when requested, rather than the constant help on more operational matters which is normally associated with buddying. Mentoring has a longer time span than buddying; informal mentoring arrangements might survive for many years.

The power of mentoring is demonstrated by the fact that many mentoring arrangements spring up informally. When I joined my current employer, there were no mentoring schemes organised. But I formed a friendship with one of the academics who interviewed me and with whom I worked. Having recruited me, he obviously felt a responsibility to help me settle in and to work out how to get the best out of the place. For me, it was very useful having someone I knew I could go and have a chat to so that I could make sense of the things that I was experiencing. I didn't call this person 'my mentor' but in actual fact that was exactly what he was.

Using buddying or mentoring

If you intend to use buddying or mentoring, you should, of course, prepare the buddy or mentor and give them the chance to think about what you expect of them. A meeting a few days before the newcomer starts to thrash out the purpose of the mentor's role is the minimum you should provide.

What socialisation techniques can you use?

- How relevant is socialisation for your vacancy?
- Which of the socialisation techniques is most suitable?
- What can you do to speed up the socialisation of newcomers to your organisation's (or department's) values and norms?

Personalisation

■ ■ ■

Whereas socialisation is the adaptation of the newcomer to the organisation, personalisation is the adaptation of the organisation to the newcomer. In most situations, personalisation is much less observable and manageable than socialisation as newcomers tend to join organisations in relatively small numbers and their influence on entire organisations is minor. Newcomers' influence on subcultures and teams, however, might be a lot more pronounced.

When a new chief executive is recruited to 'turn the company around' or a star performer is hired, the attention shifts to personalisation and to ensure that the newcomer does not 'turn native'. A good example would be when Fulham Football Club bought Bobby Moore and George Best in the 1970s. The last thing the club wanted was for the two stars to play like normal Fulham players. The club was quite successful at this, and for a season or two, Fulham was the place to watch football in England.

But this is relatively uncommon and so I shan't dwell on the subject of personalisation. Instead, in the next chapter I'll look at the eighth stage of the organisational entry process: career management. This is frequently overlooked by employers and its omission is a major reason for the attrition of staff. If you don't attend to it, you are likely to wreck all the good work you've done during the earlier stages of organisational entry.

187

SUMMARY - CHAPTER 10 *ADAPTATION*

- Socialisation is important because you want newcomers to identify with the values of the organisation.

- Buddying is the pairing up of a newcomer with a close colleague.

- Mentoring is an arrangement where the newcomer can go to a more experienced and more senior member of staff for advice.

- Buddying and mentoring should be arranged before the newcomer joins.

11
■ ■ ■

How do you keep good employees?

CHAPTER OBJECTIVES

After reading this chapter you should be able to:

- define the term 'career'
- describe how careers have changed in the last twenty years
- understand what drives the careers of your staff
- develop career action plans for your staff.

CHAPTER OVERVIEW

Organisational entry isn't just about **finding** the *right* person. It is also about **keeping** the *right* person. Up to this point, you've seen how to analyse the job and the organisation thoroughly, how to choose and use appropriate recruitment and selection techniques, and how to help the newcomer adapt to their new job. There's no point in doing all this and recruiting the best person if they leave within a few months. That's a lose-lose situation. One way to combat this is to be proactive about the career management of staff. In this chapter, I look at the advantages and disadvantages of career management, and what managers can do within their own organisational policy to help staff realise their own potential for growth and development.

What is a career?

How would you define the term 'career'?

> *How you define the term career depends on many things. One important factor is age. People who began and lived most of their working lives before the end of the 1970s are likely to talk about a planned progression of jobs within one company. If not a progression, the definition is likely to suggest permanence. For people who began work in the late 1980s, careers are likely to mean something completely different. A career might simply be a progression of separate jobs, a series of short term contracts interspersed with periods of unemployment, or a career might be a term used to describe the history of work rather than a plan of future progression. People who began work in the early 1980s were at school at a time when there was an expectation of a career waiting for them, and many had witnessed their parents in the same job or profession for all of their adult life. Perhaps more than the generations they followed or that followed them, this generation has had to struggle with the changing nature of jobs and careers. This has largely been caused by changes to the working and economic environment. I shall look at this matter first because it is a context which dominates thoughts on careers.*

190

Careers at the end of the millennium
■ ■ ■

Nowadays, there is an almost mythical image of careers. It runs something like this:

THE MYTHICAL CAREER

I offer my employer:	My employer offers me:
– commitment	– promotion prospects
– loyalty	– security
– trust	– training and development
– conformity.	– consideration.

(adapted from Herriot and Pemberton, 1995)

For most people working in Britain in the mid-1990s, this view of careers harks back to a fondly remembered age when employees wanted to help their employers because their employers wanted to help them. Both sides were willing to put in that extra effort to get things done. And it worked to the advantage of both parties. When a contract deadline was pressing, people would stay behind to get things finished. And there would be time off in lieu, or a bit extra in the Christmas bonus.

This mutual respect and loyalty was never formally written down: it existed as a psychological contract. Both parties knew the ground rules and what to expect of each other. But things have changed.

Your own career

- When did you start work?
  - before 1980
  - between 1980 and 1990
  - after 1990
- Think back to when you started work. What were your expectations of your employer and for your career?
- How have your career expectations changed?
- Think about the people you work with. Can you identify someone who started work in a different generation to you? How do you think they differ in their attitudes towards their career?

191

This reflective exercise asks you to think back to when you began your career and how your own psychological contract with your employer has changed. It is surprising how uniformly organisations have changed the psychological contract with their staff. It would be unusual if your employer was different. The reason for this seems to be related to sociological change resulting from economic and political change. When you described your current psychological contract you probably described something like this:

CAREERS IN THE 1990s

I offer my employer:
- long hours
- willing to take on responsibility
- broad range of skills
- tolerance of change, uncertainty and ambiguity.

My employer offers me:
- high pay
- rewards for performance
- a job.

(adapted from Herriot and Pemberton, 1995)

Does this psychological contract ring a bell? There are three important things to note about psychological contracts in the 1990s.

- What was previously based on a **relationship** is now based on a **transaction**. This means that nowadays employees continually consider every action to see if it is in their interests.

- Employers abused their positions of power during periods of high unemployment and breached the original agreement without consulting their workers. This has led to considerable **dissatisfaction**, **frustration**, and **anger** amongst workers many of whom believe they are being exploited because they can't go elsewhere.

- Some employers are now realising that the new psychological contract is counterproductive in the long term as they can no longer call upon the loyalty and commitment of their workforce. Furthermore, now there is greater need than ever for new ideas, innovation, and creativity. The new psychological contract forces people to 'play it safe' and reduces the likelihood of these qualities emerging.

192

Your own creativity

Pause for a moment. What was the last big risk you took at work? In what conditions would you not have taken the risk?

Understanding careers

■ ■ ■

In a wider context which forces managers always to consider the short term implications of their actions, is it useful or advisable to address the long term issues of career management? I've suggested already that innovation and creativity are likely to be associated with a more relational contract between employer and employee. In addition, organisations need committed staff to prepare, manage and handle the implications of change. And, as I mentioned at the start of the book, organisations are the people inside them. If the staff are not helped to develop and grow, what hope is there for the organisation?

The same question can be viewed from the perspective of the individual: why do people leave organisations? Research has shown that one of the most important factors causing people to look for work elsewhere is the lack of opportunities for growth and development. Overall then, even if your organisation does not address career management head on, you as a manager are well advised to consider the growth and development opportunities that you can offer your staff yourself.

Phases of careers

Attitudes to careers aren't just conditioned by the era in which people started work. Attitudes to careers are also affected by the stage of life that people are in. An American researcher, Edgar Schein, suggests that people go through three phases in their careers:

- focus on careers – usually young people
- focus on family – usually middle-aged people
- integration of career and family concerns – usually more senior people.

The exact ages of the three phases vary and are unimportant. This theory highlights that people want different things from their jobs at different stages of their lives, and that everyone is different. You cannot just assume that everyone wants a promotion or more responsibility. At times people yearn for security, at other times they will take risks to advance themselves.

At what stage of career are you and your staff?

- Focus on careers
- Focus on family
- Integration of career and family concerns

Think about your staff. For each one, try to identify at what stage their career is. What implications does this have for you?

> *The purpose of this exercise is to illustrate the point that everyone is different and needs separate consideration. If your staff are typical, you will have found that many other factors influence where people focus their attention. All you can do as a manager is to appreciate the variation, and manage each person appropriately.*

Career anchors

What shapes the way people think about their jobs? What influences the types of jobs people want to do? One answer to these questions is career anchors. A career anchor is something that binds a person to a particular career or job. Career anchors come in many forms and influence people's:

- attitudes and values
- motives and needs
- talents and abilities.

193

Your career anchors

What binds you to your job or career?

You probably thought of all manner of things; some social, others work related. On the social side, you might have mentioned proximity to friends and relations, negative equity, good salary, fondness for the location and so on. On the work related side, you might have mentioned any qualifications you have, previous work experience, other people's perceptions of your past experience, skills, and so on. In short, career anchors again stress the point that everyone is different and has different factors driving their careers.

194

My first job was as a production and systems controller for an independent record company. My main duties involved purchasing and stock control. I also did a little bit of finance including the management of royalty accounting. I left the job and moved south after a couple of years and began work in an accounting role in another company. I did this job for nine months before moving to central London to another accounting job. I hated every aspect of this job. So, after about three months, I started applying for jobs and got in touch with a number of accounting, marketing, purchasing and more general agencies. I decided that I wanted to get out of accountancy and finance. However, the only success I had was when I applied for jobs in accountancy or finance. I contacted consultants to find out why they weren't having any success getting me interviews for non-financial posts. They all gave me the same message. 'You're an accountant. And you have no experience in anything else.' No matter how much I tried to highlight my other skills, it was impossible for me to get a job outside finance, even though I had less than a year's experience working in an accounts department, I wasn't qualified, and I had other experience. In the end, it took four years to get out of accountancy and I had to move into consultancy as a headhunter and take a year out to do an MBA.

This example is interesting because it illustrates that it isn't always your own qualities that anchor you to your career. In my case, other people's perceptions of accountants severely limited my options. In fact, I found it nearly impossible to get out of the discipline once in it.

Managing careers

■ ■ ■

What can you do to help your staff plan and develop their own careers? So far, I have suggested that first of all, you need to appreciate that everyone is different and will have different objectives. This is a basic rule of management that you're surely aware of. So why mention it? Simply because this rule is particularly prominent in career management. We all tend to think that people are like ourselves and have similar aspirations and expectations. But they are not.

Other people's careers

If you get the opportunity, ask people in your department what they hope to achieve during their careers, or what their career aspirations are. Be careful though, from a manager these sorts of questions can be quite alarming. How would you react if your manager came up to you and asked 'what are your career aspirations?'

> *What can you learn from this exercise? The reason for including it was simply to make the point that people are different and they want different things from life and their career (or succession of jobs). For some it's promotion and power, for others it's high pay, for others it's security, and for others stability.*

This point suggests that it is wise to abandon thoughts that everyone is interested in a career. It is a term that carries overtones of progression upwards in organisations and of unbridled ambition. As such it entices us into thinking about careers in a particular way which isn't applicable to everyone. Instead, I'll use the term 'career outcomes' to highlight the point that everyone is different and thinks differently about the future.

A model for managing career outcomes

Given that you need to identify the different career outcome needs of everyone you manage, a model will be useful for pulling the ideas together. The model is based on the idea that people need to explore their past experience, preferences and ambitions in order to develop an awareness of their own preferred career outcomes. Once people know what these are, they can do something about them and develop a suitable action plan.

The model for career management is useful as it forces you to think about yourself and what you want to achieve. This self-awareness helps you to determine how to react to opportunities as they emerge. Many promotions and job changes arise haphazardly, without any warning, forcing people into quick decisions. The grass is always greener on the other side of the fence, and such opportunities nearly always seem more attractive than current circumstances. Sometimes people are seduced by the green grass when it is not in their best interests. If you are aware of your preferred career outcomes, you'll be better placed to assess the unplanned opportunity when it appears.

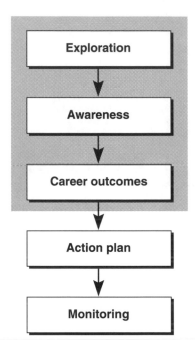

Fig 11.1 A career planning process

Exploration, awareness and career outcomes

People don't know themselves as well as they think they do. Most people never sit down and learn from their own experiences.

I occasionally run career management sessions for managers. First, I ask them to describe their own careers in the form of a picture or diagram. Then I ask them to share their picture with another manager. Finally, they work through a series of questions that help them think about their own careers to date, what they want from their careers, and how to form an action plan. More often than not, the response is something along these lines, 'that's the first time I've really thought about my career', 'what a mess my career is – nothing's been planned', 'I now know what I want from life'. The purpose of relating this example is not to sell career management courses, but to illustrate the point that most people haven't ever sat down and thought about their career, and, consequently, don't have any clear idea about what they want to achieve.

These career management sessions also demonstrate the first stage of the model: how exploring your own past and present helps you to develop an awareness of yourself and your circumstances. Once you are aware of your talents, skills, ambitions, etc., you are better placed to think about:

- what you want to achieve from your life and career
- whether your preferred outcomes are realistic
- what other outcomes would bring you satisfaction
- what you have to do to be able to achieve your preferred outcomes.

197

A little later in the chapter you'll find a series of activities that will help you understand your own preferred career outcomes better. Obviously, you can also use the questions to help someone else understand their own career better.

Action plan

Once you've worked out what you want to achieve, the next stage is to develop an action plan. Ideally, you should look at actions in the short, medium, and long term. The purpose of this is to give yourself targets to aim for and specific action for the immediate future.

Monitoring

It is too easy to develop an action plan, do a few things, and then forget all about it. Your career management action plan is too important for that, and you should revisit it on a regular basis, say every three months, to check progress and see whether it needs amending in the light of new information and the effects of actions.

Opportunities for career development

How and when can you help people with their careers? There are many occasions apart from the obvious informal discussion. Some of the more formalised methods include:

- development centres (assessment centres used to spot and develop talent)
- structured activities such as specially designed workbooks and questionnaires
- in-tray exercises
- questionnaires
- role plays
- appraisal interviews.

All these formal methods are opportunities for you, the manager, to help the individual develop a better awareness of their capabilities and preferences. The appraisal interview is particularly important because in many organisations it is the only time when a manager is explicitly asked to focus on the development of the employee.

A structured intervention for career management

198

Each of the techniques are more or less appropriate to particular circumstances. So, rather than analyse each type of opportunity, I feel it is more useful to describe a more general process of career management that you can use in a number of different ways and which is suitable in many circumstances.

Stage 1: Exploration

What has gone before? What is happening now? Why did I choose what I chose? What choices do I have? These are just some of the questions that can help people understand their careers to date. But there are more interesting ways of reviewing a career.

- **Autobiography** – write the story of your career to date. What were your choices and what influenced them? How did events outside work affect your decisions? What career anchors did you put down? and so on.
- **Career review** – an alternative method is to create a record or list of each of your jobs accompanied by the things you liked and disliked about each, and the things you did well and badly.
- **Career mapping** – drawing a picture of your career can be most informative and very quick. The idea is that by drawing a picture of your career and then explaining it to another person, you surface many of the key issues that you have confronted. Use analogies to construct the drawing. A good example is to draw a career as a river with its ebbs and flows, rapids, waterfalls, wider calmer slower sections. Items on the bank are the

factors affecting your decisions. Other examples are aeroplane flights, walks, pinball machines, and chemical processes. All are journeys with a definite start point and a destination – even though the destination won't yet have been reached.

Your career as a picture

Try to draw a picture of your own career.

Now that you've drawn an image of your own career, you need to talk it through with someone you can trust. Try to focus on your choice points and the factors that contributed to your decisions. Once you've explained your diagram, try to answer the following questions. Check your answers to the questions with your listener so that they can see whether or not you have been consistent and realistic in your plans.

199

Career exploration

- What were your favourite and least liked subjects at school?
- What subjects did you do best and worst in at school?
- What other activities were you involved in at school?
- What were your favourite and least liked subjects at college?
- What subjects did you do best and worst in at college?
- What other activities were you involved in at college?
- What career anchors can you identify from your school and college activities?
- How did you choose your first job?
- What did (do) you like most and least about your favourite job?
- What did you achieve in this job?
- How well did (are) you perform(ing) on the job?
- What factors contributed to high performance in this job?
- What career anchors did you put down in this job?
- At what stage of your career were you when you did this job?
- What caused you to leave this job?
- What did (do) you like least and most about your worst job?
- What did you achieve in this job?
- How well did (are) you perform(ing) on the job?
- What factors contributed to high performance in this job?
- What career anchors did you put down in this job?
- At what stage of your career were you when you did this job?
- What caused you to leave this job?

How does your professional life fit in with your personal life?
How important are each of the following aspects of your life?
How do they influence your attitudes and decisions?

- Family life
- Leisure and recreational pursuits
- Community activities
- Religious/spiritual activities

Stage 2: Awareness

The next activity gives you the opportunity to make sense of the data surfaced during your exploration.

Career awareness

Look at the information which emerged during your career exploration.

- Can you identify any common themes or career anchors?
- What incidents or evidence are related to each of the career anchors?
- Describe your current relationships with family and friends. How do these relationships affect your career choices?

Stage 3: Career outcomes

You should now have gathered a lot of information about your career and preferences. The next thing to do is to translate this into career outcomes. So that you can develop realistic and specific action plans, you need to think about short, medium and long term objectives.

Career outcomes

What are the lessons coming out of your awareness?
- In broad terms, what do you want to achieve in life?
- What would make you happy?
- What alternative career outcomes would satisfy you?
- What are your long term (more than 5 years) preferred career outcomes?
- In the long term what career outcomes do you want to avoid?
- What are your medium term (2–5 years) preferred career outcomes?
- In the medium term what career outcomes do you want to avoid?
- What are your short term (less than 2 years) preferred career outcomes?
- In the short term what career outcomes do you want to avoid?
- What do you want to achieve in your current job?
- How do these ambitions fit in with the rest of your life?
- Describe your **ideal** job. Be specific about the roles, tasks, objectives, culture, environment, people, values, rewards, and so on.

Stage 4: Action plans

Having outlined your objectives, the next stage is to plan how to achieve them.

Career action plan

Look at your description of your ideal job.

- What are the probable job title and location of this job?
- If you were to apply for this post, what would be your strengths and weaknesses?
- What experience do you need to gain to be a credible applicant?
- What qualifications do you need to get?
- What skills do you need to develop?
- What knowledge do you need to acquire?
- What relationships must you cultivate?
- What other activities would help you?
- Look at your action plan.
  - What actions can you do in the next week? Be specific.
  - What actions can you do in the next month? Be specific.
  - What actions can you do in the next six months? Be specific.
  - Who can help you with your action plan?

201

Stage 5: Monitoring

You must plan how you will monitor your action plan. In the next chapter, I'll look at a device called a control loop. You can adapt this idea to monitor your career progression.

SUMMARY – CHAPTER 11 *ATTRITION*

- Careers means different things to different people.

- Careers need to be managed if you are to keep your best employees.

- In the last 20 years careers have changed a lot. They are now based on a transaction rather than a relationship.

- During their lives, people's careers go through phases.

- People are limited in their options by the career anchors they put down.

- When planning a career, ask the subject to explore their past, other events, family, and social life to give them an awareness of what they wish to achieve in their working life.

12
. . .
How can you be sure you got it right?

CHAPTER OBJECTIVES

After reading this chapter you should be able to:
- explain how the control loop works
- use the control loop to monitor the performance of your organisational entry process
- identify and correct mistakes for subsequent organisational entry exercises.

CHAPTER OVERVIEW

This is a short chapter that concentrates on one issue: analysing the organisational entry process to ascertain its effectiveness. This is done by using a control loop, which helps you compare the performance of the process to the standards and objectives that you set at the start of the search for a new member of staff. I explain how the model works before demonstrating how it can be applied to organisational entry. At the end of the chapter, I look at how you can learn from previous organisational entry episodes.

When it all goes wrong

∎ ∎ ∎

If you have followed through the ideas in this book to find and keep a new member of staff, you would be most unfortunate to recruit the wrong person. But sometimes this does happen. If it has happened to you, what should you do about it? Assuming that you've already carried out suitable introduction and socialisation practices, your next step would be to look at training and development options. When this proves fruitless, you've tried everything that anyone could reasonably expect.

Although you have a responsibility to those you recruit, there comes a time when you need to cut your losses. It is easy to get into an escalating spiral of commitment: 'we've already invested so much, we can't give up now'. But when it has all gone wrong, it's better for both parties to separate and put the extra effort into managing the separation with dignity. Remember that no one's to blame for the failure (as long as you've been thorough and fair), but the organisation has a responsibility to the individual it invited to join.

If you find yourself in this situation you must learn from the experience. What caused you to recruit the wrong person? What can you do differently to make sure it doesn't happen again?

The control loop

∎ ∎ ∎

In this book, I've shown you how to construct selection criteria from a job analysis, and how you can recruit a person based on these selection criteria. I've suggested that you consider how to help the newcomer adapt and identify with the new employer. All well and good, but have you actually managed to recruit someone who is performing well in the job, gets satisfaction from it, and is motivated to perform better? If yes, do you know how you achieved this? If no, do you know what went wrong and how you will prevent a similar mistake happening again?

The control loop is a managerial tool that can be used to plan how you will monitor a process or procedure. It can be portrayed as a diagram (see overleaf) or as a process.

The control loop is similar to the rational decision making model described earlier, in that the first three stages set standards (or criteria), measure something, and then compare it to the standards. The control loop differs because it offers you three courses of action depending on whether you meet standards or not.

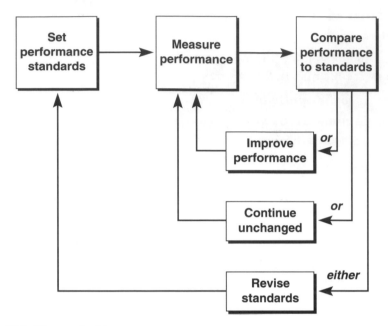

Fig 12.1 The control loop

THE CONTROL LOOP

1   Set performance standards.
2   Measure performance.
3   Compare performance to standards.

If standards have been met:
● continue unchanged and continue to monitor performance.

If standards have not been met, either:
● take action to improve performance, or
● revise the standards.

Clearly, the control loop is highly applicable to the organisational entry process. It can be used to look at the performance of an individual worker, or to monitor the performance of the entire organisational entry process. It is this second use that I want to look at in more detail.

Controlling the organisational entry process

Stage 1: Set performance standards

This task brings our discussion full circle: what do you want to achieve when you set out to recruit someone? In chapter 1, I suggested that, in most circumstances, you want to find someone who:

- **performs** well
- is highly **motivated**
- is **committed** to the organisation
- gets **satisfaction** from their work.

You may also want to achieve a number of subsidiary objectives, such as the fair and efficient administration of the process, or the reduction of training costs. Do you agree? Are these your objectives when recruiting someone?

What are your objectives?

205

Now that you've read most of this book, what do you hope to achieve when recruiting someone? How will you judge whether or not the organisational entry exercise was a success?

Stage 2: Measure performance

Measuring performance is such a large topic that it could easily fill this book. As a result, I cannot give the subject the space or treatment it deserves. Instead, I'll try and capture the key things that you need to know to be able to measure the effectiveness of your organisational entry process. The information you need can either be:

- quantitative (numerical content)
- qualitative (word content).

Both these types of information are important and neither is better than the other. It is simply that sometimes numbers are more appropriate than words, or vice versa. For example, it is more appropriate to measure the turnover of staff using numbers, and to use words to describe psychological states such as satisfaction or anxiety levels.

How do you gather information regarding your objectives? There are several common ways of doing so:

- observation and involvement
- questioning and discussion
- routine statistics

- specially produced statistics
- regular reports
- exception reports.

Each of these methods has its own strengths and weaknesses:

- **observation and involvement** – can give you a rich picture, but, as discussed earlier, the drawback of observation is the amount of time it consumes

- **questioning and discussion** – are useful for determining psychological states such as commitment and satisfaction, although you'll want to check that actions match words

- **routine statistics** – your organisation may already have information relevant to your objectives, especially for performance related matters – these are particularly useful for spotting trends

- **specially produced statistics** – the drawback is time, effort and the expertise required, but these can help you measure key objectives that are frequently ignored

- **regular reports** – obviously useful, but it all depends on how good the reports are

- **exception reports** – vitally important for assessing organisational entry objectives, but don't always assume that 'no news is good news' – remember that exception reports can come in a verbal as well as a written format and sometimes a combination of both; 'here's my notice'.

How can you measure your organisational entry objectives?

Describe how you will measure each of the organisational entry objectives you listed earlier.

Stage 3: Compare performance to standards

This stage rather speaks for itself. It is simply a matter of comparing your performance measures against your standards and assessing whether or not the standards have been met.

Option 1: Continue unchanged   If all the outcome measures are being met, then you continue unchanged. But you don't just leave it there. You want to try to form an understanding of the factors contributing to your success. Did you make any key decisions that contributed to it? Did you do anything differently from previous organisational entry episodes? If so, what impact did these changes make? If you have the time, write up your findings to inform future organisational entry episodes that you might have to carry out. Checking performance once doesn't mean that the process has finished. The control loop model is ongoing and you should regularly check to see whether your standards are still being met.

Option 2: Revise standards   Where the standards and targets are not being met, you have two courses of action: either you change the standards and targets, or you need to take corrective action. Revising your standards is quite a radical step. It will mean that your objectives were not realistic. Is this the case? If you decide to do nothing when something needs to be done, then you are implicitly changing the standards and targets.

Option 3: Take corrective action   When you spot a failure to meet standards, you should obviously try to put things right. This can be tackled on two fronts. First, you can take corrective action to improve the performance of people actually doing the job. Typical remedies would include more training, more socialisation events, or simply discussing the problem with the newcomer. The second front you need to analyse is the organisational entry process itself. Do you know what caused the problem to occur? The following questions illustrate the sort of things that might have gone wrong:

207

- were appropriate methods used to analyse the job?
- after the job analysis, did you have an accurate picture of the job?
- did the job description accurately portray the job?
- did the selection criteria properly reflect the key qualities required to do the job?
- did the recruitment techniques attract a pool of suitably qualified applicants?
- were selection techniques chosen to examine people against the selection criteria?
- were the selection techniques performed effectively?
- did the selectors make a fair decision?
- did the newcomer experience dysfunctional disorientation when they arrived?
- were introduction and socialisation strategies effective?

> **Before starting out on a fresh organisational entry campaign you need to understand the strengths and weaknesses of previous campaigns.**
>
> - **What was effective?**
> - **Where did you go wrong?**
> - **How can you improve?**

Improving organisational entry

Think of someone at work who, since joining, has been less effective than expected. Can you identify any flaws in the organisational entry process that contributed to the decision to appoint a less than effective person?

How might the process have been improved so that a more suitable person was appointed?

> It is important to realise that when a less than effective person is appointed, it is a failure of everyone involved in the organisational entry process. The organisation is as much, if not more, to blame as the applicant. There are many interventions that managers can use to take corrective action. These have been discussed earlier in this book.

A reminder

When monitoring the performance of your organisational entry process, remember to monitor it for fairness. This was covered towards the end of chapter 2.

SUMMARY – CHAPTER 12 *AUDIT*

- A control loop is a simple management tool for monitoring the effectiveness of a process or procedure.

- A control loop has three stages:
  - set performance standards
  - measure performance
  - compare performance to standards.

- If standards have been met, continue unchanged and continue to monitor performance.

- If standards have not been met, either:
  - take action to improve performance, or
  - revise the standards.

- Before starting out on a fresh organisational entry campaign, you need to understand the strengths and weaknesses of previous campaigns:
  - were they effective?
  - where did you go wrong?
  - how can you improve?

13

. . .

Bringing the ideas together

OVERVIEW

This book has covered much ground. I started by looking at the ideas underpinning effective organisational entry. This highlighted the need to consider how well applicants fit the job and the organisation. Then I looked at all the stages of organisational entry from the initial assessment that you need to recruit someone all the way through to the introduction, socialisation, and career management of newcomers. Finally, I looked at a management tool that can help you monitor and control the effectiveness of the whole process.

REVIEW

In the introduction to this book, I related the tale of the hapless Pascale and Rob in their attempts to find a new member of staff. When you first read the short case study, you probably spotted many of their mistakes. But now that you've read this book, you'll probably spot many more.

How much have I learnt?

Return to the introduction in this book. Read the case study featuring Pascale and Rob again. As you read through the case study, note the mistakes that Pascale and Rob made.

For each of the mistakes you noticed, how might they have done better?

You might have spotted the following mistakes.

- *Pascale's thought 'what is it now?' about the relative newcomer (five months) and John's comment 'I don't think I fit in around here' both suggest that Pascale hasn't given time or thought to the adjustment and socialisation of newcomers.*
- *Good internal candidates were passed over because 'they're even more indispensable in their current jobs'.*
- *The previous point and future events also illustrated the failure to think about the careers of people in the team.*
- *There was no analysis of the job or the organisational environment.*
- *No selection criteria were developed.*
- *They repeated the mistakes of previous organisational entry episodes: 'it didn't take us long to recruit John last time, let's do the same again'.*
- *They didn't consider recruitment alternatives.*
- *Shortlisting was haphazard.*
- *They didn't consider selection alternatives.*
- *They didn't prepare their interviews or think about their format or structure. They certainly didn't decide what topics each interviewer would cover.*
- *Haphazard selection criteria were developed after interviewing, and were not based on any sort of organisational entry analysis. Rob certainly had no idea of these points when interviewing.*
- *Subjective judgements about fitting in were made.*
- *Nothing was done to test the skills and abilities of applicants. It would have been easy to develop an analogous test to assess their accounting skills.*
- *They chose the 'least bad' applicant.*
- *The manner and lack of professionalism of the interviews communicated itself to the best candidate who rejected the job offer.*
- *There was no attempt to give any of the applicants a realistic preview of the job.*
- *They appointed Juliet who was only acceptable 'at a pinch'.*
- *There was no negotiation or discussion with Juliet to agree or communicate the organisation's expectations of her at work.*
- *Useless unstructured references were requested.*
- *No thought was given to introduction or socialisation.*
- *No thought was given to the effect of the newcomer on existing members of staff.*

This exercise illustrates the development you've made in reading this book. Think back to when you first read the case study. Did you spot half the mistakes you spotted this time? If you've noticed most of these mistakes, you're well prepared to be effective at organisational entry yourself.

Development

■ ■ ■

Many of the ideas I've covered might be quite new to you, others you'll already have known about. It is worth spending a couple of minutes thinking about these new ideas so that they don't get lost.

What have you learnt from reading this book?

- What are the key things you have learnt from reading this book?
- What will you do differently now?

A SUMMARY – FINDING AND KEEPING THE *RIGHT* PEOPLE

- Organisational entry begins when you have a genuine need to recruit some-one and ends when the new recruit is working effectively and is fully inte-grated into the organisation.

- When recruiting someone you need to think about how well they fit the job and how well they fit the organisation.

- It is unlawful to discriminate against applicants because of their gender, race, or because they are married.

- All organisational entry decisions should be rational decisions: i.e. objective and systematic.

- Before starting the organisational entry process you should think about the organisation's and the team's staffing requirements in the short and long term.

- The goal of organisational entry analysis is to develop selection criteria that capture the key skills and abilities required to do the job and fit into the organisation.

- You want to attract a small number of suitably qualified applicants.

- Publicity material about vacancies should be targeted.

- 'Tell it like it is.'

- All selection decisions should be based on the selection criteria.

- The manner of an interview is important in shaping attitudes to work.

- Spend time talking with the applicant to agree terms and conditions.

- Manage the introduction of the newcomer into the organisation.

- Help members of your team to identify their preferred career outcomes and to develop action plans to achieve them.

- Monitor your organisational entry exercises: keep getting it right.

211

A final thought

■ ■ ■

Commonly, managers think recruitment and selection are finished when their offer letter is accepted. This view is typical of the traditional idea of organisational entry, which places all the emphasis on the selection phase of the process. As this book has demonstrated, there is much more to organisational entry than that. This point is illustrated by a metaphor that I originally wrote for another book (Billsberry, 1996).

A gardener wakes up one morning to find that, overnight, thieves have stolen the ornamental pot containing a number of plants that formed the centrepiece in a prize winning border (headhunters have a habit of doing this). As the BBC programme *Gardener's World* is due to visit in a few months to film the garden in full bloom, he has to do something about it. He needs to find a replacement.

As he stands, rather dismayed, looking at the border, he realises that he has several options. His initial reaction is to rush to the garden centre to purchase another ornamental pot, replant it in a similar fashion and thereby recreate what had existed. But he pauses; he has a 'development opportunity'. Could he make things even better? Have the thieves done him a favour? That pot had always been a bit of a problem, it had come with the garden and had always seemed such a formidable, if impressive, thing. Perhaps a different type of centrepiece; maybe a flowering tree? But now the pot's gone, the other plants in the border seem much more prominent and much more attractive. Perhaps, rather than finding another centrepiece, he could replace the pot with something that helps the others stand out even more. Eventually, he chooses this option and decides to buy some smaller shrubs that will enhance the other plants in the border. His choice is limited by the nature of the soil and the sunlight and so he carries out a lot of analysis to identify suitable plants.

Where to buy the plants? He has several options, but as time is tight, he decides to get in the car and go straight to his local garden centre which he knows has the sort of plants he's looking for. At the garden centre, the experienced gardener chooses his new shrubs quite easily as he knows what he's looking for. He takes more time choosing the right fertiliser and compost so that the new plants will bed in quickly.

Before planting the new shrubs he spends a lot of time preparing the border and getting the conditions just right. During the first week of planting, he attends daily to the new plants making sure they are correctly watered and haven't been attacked by predatory birds. Over the next two months he works with the plants every week to ensure that they develop in the way that he wants, to complement the other flowers in the border.

A few months later when the *Gardener's World* film crew appears, the gardener and the producer discuss the border. It has changed a great deal since the producer first saw the garden and decided to feature it. They both agree that the border is just as good as before; perhaps even better.

213

Further reading

■ ■ ■

Anderson, N. and Shackleton, V. (1993) *Successful Selection Interviewing*, Oxford: Blackwell

Billsberry, J. (1996) *The Effective Manager: Perspectives and Illustrations*, London: Sage

Clark, T.A.R. (1995) *Managing Consultants*, Buckingham: Open University Press

Hackman, J.R. and Oldham, G.R. (1980) *Work Redesign*, Reading, MA: Addison-Wesley

Herriot, P. and Pemberton C. (1995) *New Deals*, Chichester: Wiley

Kline, P. (1993) *The Handbook of Psychological Testing*, London: Routledge

Parkinson, C.N. (1958) *Parkinson's Law*, London: Penguin

Pearn, M. and Kandola, R. (1993) *Job Analysis: A Manager's Guide*, 2nd edn., London: Institute of Personnel Management

Robbins, S.P. (1996) *Organizational Behavior: Concepts, Controversies, Applications*, 7th edn. Englewood Cliffs, NJ: Prentice Hall

Schein, E.H. (1978) *Career Dynamics: Matching Individual and Organizational Needs*, Reading, MA: Addison-Wesley

Skeats, J. (1991) *Successful Induction*, London: Kogan Page.

Smith, M. and Robertson, I.T. (1993) *The Theory and Practice of Systematic Personnel Selection*, 2nd edn., Basingstoke: Macmillan

Wanous, J.P. (1992) *Organizational Entry*, 2nd edn., Reading, MA: Addison-Wesley.

Useful addresses

■ ■ ■

Advisory, Conciliation and Arbitration Service (ACAS), 27 Wilton Street, London SW1X 7AZ (0171 210 3000)

British Psychological Society, St. Andrew's House, 48 Princess Road East, Leicester LE1 7DR (0116 254 9568)

Commission for Racial Equality, Elliot House, 10-12 Allington Street, London SW1E 5EH (0171 828 7022)

Equal Opportunities Commission, Overseas House, Quay Street, Manchester M3 3HN (0161 833 9244)

Institute of Personnel and Development, IPD House, Camp Road, Wimbledon, London SW19 4UX (0181 971 9000)

The Open University, Walton Hall, Milton Keynes MK7 6AA (01908 274066)

The Royal Association for Disability and Rehabilitation (RADAR), Unit 12, City Forum, 250 City Road, London EC1V 8AF (0171 250 3222)

Index

■ ■ ■

217

219